Advance Praise for
Leading from the Roots:
Nature Inspired Leadership Lessons for Today's World
by Dr. Kathleen Allen

In an era of sound bites, top ten lists and "pointers" on leadership, Dr. Allen has made it her life's work to understand the "why" behind great leadership practices. This perspective gives us the context necessary to understand organizational behavior on a whole new level. *Leading from the Roots* is not about the quick fix, it is about making us think holistically about organizations through the lens of the most successful system there has ever been, nature. By analyzing the natural world and applying its lessons to the complex landscape of organizations, Dr. Allen has broken the code on why different leadership techniques work and how they come together to create great results. A must-read for any enlightened leader.

-Brian Myres,
CEO MYRES CONSULTING, LLC

When we create a world of generous organizations, everyone thrives. Dr. Kathleen Allen takes the reader on a journey to this world by painting a landscape of how high-functioning, generous organizations look based on the longest-running R&D lab on the planet—nature. Drawing on her extensive experience in organizational development and leadership coaching, she uses her keen ability to quiet the ego and listen to nature's core principles of life to then translate them into relevant and impactful strategies for leadership and organizational evolution to generous systems.

-Daniel Lawse, Principal, Co-founder,
and Chief Century Thinker at Verdis Group.

Dr. Allen brings reason to the service of the passion that I feel for Nature's wisdom and power. I maintain that every lesson for living, learning, serving, and leading is either written indelibly in or is compellingly inspired by Nature. Dr. Allen confirms my strongly held sentiments, backing my premises with reference to a body of knowledge (her admirable bibliography) and decades of her own experience identifying and applying nature's lessons and inspiration through research, consulting, advising, and leading. Both natural systems and human enterprises evolve. Dr. Allen tells us how to nudge, model, and encourage deliberate evolution toward generous organizations.

One simple extract distills all that Dr. Allen presents so beautifully in *Leading from the Roots: Nature Inspired Leadership Lessons for Today's World.* "We are turning to nature as our mentor, model, and muse to inform the way we understand organizations and leadership and our aspirations for what our organizations can become." I say Amen and Hallelujah!

-Steve Jones, Author, Nature Based Leadership
and Nature-Inspired Learning and Leading. Great Blue Heron, CEO.

"Nature runs on generosity." What a profound concept. In this book, Kathy Allen, inspired by nature, inspires each of us to unleash our capacity to explore living systems in *Leading from the Roots* and growing generous organizations. Throughout this thought-provoking book, Allen uses nature and biomimicry principles, metaphors, and mindsets to nudge the boundaries of leadership thinking and practices towards a higher shared purpose—leading a generous organization.

-Dr. Cynthia Cherrey, President & CEO
International Leadership Association

Leading from the Roots provides a powerful new way of thinking about organizations as living systems and delivers practical leadership frameworks for individuals to learn how to unleash the energy and create innovative, effective teams. Dr. Kathleen Allen has identified the power of changing the metaphor of an organization from a machine that needs to be controlled to a living system that has the capacity to sustainably evolve. Taking lessons from complex biological systems, Dr. Allen articulates the key elements that must be present and how to apply this in an organizational context. Whether bringing a fresh approach to executive transitions with the metaphor of 'living bridges', reminding us of the power and necessity of transparently managing tensions, or helping us ask ourselves what do we need to relinquish to move forward, Dr. Allen helps us to adapt to our rapidly changing opportunities. *Leading from the Roots* is not only thought-provoking, but offers valuable exercises and questions to help us think and act differently. Leveraging the natural tendencies of living systems, we can increase the vibrancy and sustainability of our organizations and the people who power them.

-Anne Bonaparte, CEO Appthority

Allen's book challenged and strengthened my lessons of leadership. The change from asking "What can I control?" to "What can I unleash?" is just the beginning of viewing and leading more effectively with an understanding and acceptance of leadership in organizations that are dynamic, unpredictable and chaotic.

How is it that leadership in so many organizations just gets "it" wrong and organizations and people suffer? Allen makes the case that there are valuable leadership lessons from learning from nature's living systems and its diversity, resiliency and adaptability.

As a leader, I subscribe to the importance of vision, inputs, assessment and goals. Allen's work challenges me to consider the leadership lessons of nature by asking myself what I can let go off, unleash and trust. It's a new lens and perspective on leadership—and there's no "un-ringing this bell" after reading this book. Your leadership understanding will be both challenged and strengthened after reading.

-Jim Hoolihan, CEO Industrial Lubricant

Leading from the Roots fills a void in leadership literature that you are sure to find useful. Dr. Allen challenges us to lead organizations in a different way— no longer relying on traditional models, but using nature's principles to create transformation. Brilliant!

If you are interested in taking your leadership into the 21st century and beyond, Leading from the Roots: Nature Inspired Leadership Lessons for Today's World is a must-read! Dr. Allen unpacks a unique and impactful approach to creating the organizations we all want to work in.

-Armando Camacho, CEO Opportunity Partners

As the CEO of a mission-driven organization, I'm often struggling to unlock the potential of the talented people who are drawn to the work we do. Kathy Allen has given me and my peers the gift of a new way of considering this puzzle, using the compelling metaphor of the natural world to help us see how we can unleash the passions of those around us and the organizations we serve.

-Phillip Henderson, CEO Surdna Foundation

Kathy Allen's singular application of biomimicry pushes the "growth edge" of human thought about leadership, organizations, and community development. Most of us enter this terrain with much confusion and discouraging bumps and scrapes. Yet there, holding a lamplight on the far side of the room, is Kathy illuminating a path forward. In this way, *Leading from the Roots* points to an evolutionary leap in human self-understanding. It will help us derive a more abundant, integrated, and life-giving future: starting with ourselves, extending through our work, and serving our immediate and global communities. Thank you, Kathy.

-Matthew Rezac, Sherwood Foundation

There are too few books that explore leadership of purpose. Through the metaphor of nature Kathleen offers us an exciting vision and argument: *Leading from the Roots: Nature Inspired Leadership Lessons for Today's World* is rooted in an ecology of reciprocation and embedded in evolving open systems. At a time in which our consumptive organizations and societies have led to us to the ecological brink this book is most timely and apposite.

-Professor Steve Kempster,
Lancaster University Management School, UK

Dr. Kathleen Allen in *Leading from the Roots: Nature Inspired Leadership Lessons for Today's World* has expanded on the premise that leadership is relational to include a keen analysis of living systems and their impact on leadership development and theory. As the author explains, living systems embrace a diversity of perspectives, and are inclusive of constant experimentation and growth, always seeking to build more vibrant organizations. Dr. Allen believes if we take the approach nature encourages, we will construct stronger and healthier organizations in the long-term even if the journey may be a bit turbulent at times.

Dr. Allen recognizes that effective leadership is never simple; it is complex and dynamic often resulting in challenge, conflict, change and resolution resulting in the creation of much more adaptive, stable and generous organizations. Not only do most of us desire to work in these generous organizations, they promise to be more sustainable and productive in the long-term.

In this very insightful, creative book, Dr. Allen encourages all of us interested in leadership to be much more observant of the world around us in order to learn from nature what the natural process of leadership development really is. She has created a very innovative analysis of leadership based on a practical appreciation of life, change, conflict, evolution, and resolution. This is a very important contribution furthering the exploration and discussion of leadership development. It is a must-read for students and scholars of leadership!

-Roger H. Sublett, Ph.D.,
President Union Institute & University

This book is a must-read for organizational leaders who are not only committed to their mission, but equally to creating a workplace that attracts and retains the brightest and the best professionals fully enabled to meet that mission.

-Caryl Stern, President & CEO UNICEF USA

If you are a leader and want to deepen your impact, read this book and hire her as a personal coach! My coaching relationship with Kathy has expanded my worldview and has enriched my leadership practice.

-Caren Dewar, Executive Director,
Urban Land Institute Minnesota USA

Kathleen Allen has transformed the landscape of leadership in this landmark book. It is filled with rich organic imagery infused with a sound knowledge of biology, social systems, and human and organizational development. It provides an immense amount of wisdom gleaned from decades of experience of working in the terrain of leadership and the cultural soil in which it was and is rooted.

We are in a period of incomprehensible change and a degree of complexity rarely experienced in the history of humankind. Not only does Allen capture this complexity and the major shift it is inducing, she provides the reader with detailed descriptions of the impact on our thinking and behavior, and provides a strong argument for why there is a need and urgency to undergo a transition in the thinking of all leadership professionals.

This is a profoundly different view of reality in which top/down leadership must not remain as the dominant paradigm in the field of leadership. The consequences are spelled out in depth and the rewards for changing compelling. Her developmental approach, which is analogous to the way nature operates, addresses such questions of why and how leaders need to embrace diversity and sees the systems in which we work as living, ever changing, connected organisms capable of listening to feedback, engaging in self-correction, and retaining flexibility in ways that are innovative yet resilient. Our view of systems and the interventions we bring to them really matter.

The reader is not left without guidance as to how to begin to grow new ways of thinking and leading in the new reality. Each chapter offers behavioral changes for consideration and at the end a set of questions that further the conversation about the role of leaders in creating spaces and practices for the evolution of generous organizations. Allen's generosity throughout the book reflects the beliefs and ideas she lives and works by, providing readers with challenging and gracious space in which to learn and grow.

-Katherine Tyler Scott, Principle Ki ThoughtBridge; Board Chair
International Leadership Association

Leading from the Roots

Nature Inspired Leadership Lessons for Today's World

Leading from the Roots

Nature Inspired Leadership Lessons for Today's World

Dr. Kathleen E. Allen

NEW YORK

LONDON • NASHVILLE • MELBOURNE • VANCOUVER

Leading from the Roots

Nature Inspired Leadership Lessons for Today's World.

Published in New York, New York, by Morgan James Publishing. Morgan James and The Entrepreneurial Publisher are trademarks of Morgan James, LLC.
www.MorganJamesPublishing.com

The Morgan James Speakers Group can bring authors to your live event. For more information or to book an event visit The Morgan James Speakers Group at www.TheMorganJamesSpeakersGroup.com.

ISBN 9781683508496 paperback
ISBN 9781683508502 eBook
Library of Congress Control Number: 2017917473

Cover Design by:
Megan Whitney
Creative Ninja Designs

Interior Design by:
Paul Curtis

In an effort to support local communities, raise awareness and funds, Morgan James Publishing donates a percentage of all book sales for the life of each book to Habitat for Humanity Peninsula and Greater Williamsburg.

Get involved today! Visit
www.MorganJamesBuilds.com

Table of Contents

Dedication

To my parents, who believed we should always leave things better then we find them and nurtured my love of nature.

And to the Millennials, may this book help you become leaders of organizations that create more and consume less.

Acknowledgements

A writer never really writes alone. While we may be the one sitting day after day writing in front of our computer, we have the company of many colleagues, clients, friends, and family who have influenced us and helped us evolve our thinking and applications.

I am very lucky to have so many clients and colleagues who have joined me in my consulting work to experiment with the ideas in this book.

I would like to thank Daniel Lawse and Matthew Rezac who share my interest in applying biomimicry to organizations and communities. I would like to acknowledge Marci Heerman and Carol Pearson, who along with Daniel and Matt, gave me feedback on drafts at various stages along the way. My friend Maxine Barnett has read and reread many versions of my whole book. I am deeply grateful for the time and attention she gave to this project.

This book wouldn't be what it is without the help of my editor Megan Scribner. Her wonderful ability to see how the whole narrative could be stronger by eliminating a sentence here or moving a paragraph there (as well as her attention to technical editing) was a great asset in bringing my ideas to life.

Special thanks go to my brother David Erskine, who has helped me with marketing and selling this book. His skills have been invaluable to me.

I would also like to acknowledge my colleagues at Morgan James Publishing for all their help and support getting this book published.

Foreword

I appreciate the publication of *Leading from the Roots* on many levels. First, it exemplifies how humanity is moving beyond the "man and nature" idea of conquering the natural world and beyond our fascination with the wonders of technology that has rendered us more and more robotic. Now we are beginning to understand that people are part of nature, and yes, that nature is smarter than we are. Of course, nature does not speak or write great books, but from it comes all the marvels of living things and bodies that function in so many ways—blood circulating, food digesting, wounds healing, etc.—without our minds controlling the action. It is a great thing to have a book that can help us replicate some of this living system intelligence in what we do; starting with the insight that learning from nature is a wise thing to do.

Second, I am grateful for this book for what it teaches me about leadership, so much so, that I wish I'd had it to read years ago when I first became a leader. Dr. Allen has taken living systems thinking and boiled it down to a manageable blue print for leading in a whole new way. Yes, pieces of this approach can be found here and there, as she acknowledges while integrating these into a coherent and valuable whole. And, third, in this strange time in history, where time to think is scarce, she has managed to hone down her ideas into concise form and offered them in easy to grasp chunks.

And fourth, Allen's book provides a major and needed contribution to leadership theory. While "great man" approaches to leadership are holding on in its twilight years, Allen's work provides a missing piece to more contemporary theories. She contributes to authentic and situational leadership theory by helping us recognize why we need to be authentic and emotionally intelligent as we work with organizations and other living systems. Most of all, she expands transformational leadership theory from bringing out the best in the change makers, to bringing out the best in the whole human system, including each and every one of us involved within an organization and in its larger context.

I am currently writing about the US and about how we might reunite as a people to address the problems of the twenty-first century. Allen's work has made me wonder about what it would be like to think about our economic system as a living system. For example:

- *Could we figure out what relationships are resulting in the huge and growing income gap, and what could be done to create greater fairness and justice in the US today?*
- *How could the US become a more generous country to all groups within it and to the larger world? And how could each of us, as citizens, become more generous, first by recognizing what is ours to give and then giving it, in gratitude for what we receive?*
- *What would it be like if we applied living system ideas to education? Could we figure out how schools could be configured so that more students consistently learned and fewer dropped out, utilizing the full resources involved—in students as well as teachers and in the larger social context?*
- *How could we use Allen's approach in neighborhood redevelopment and in corporate social responsibility?*

The potential applications of living system ideas are endless. Thinking back on a recent leadership challenge, I'm also taken with how important it is for leaders to avoid buying into false polarities. In times of stress and conflict, people begin to cluster their issues around two opposing premises which then promote conflict. We had this in the Cold War, and we have it in the current idea of an American Culture War, and in most organizational change efforts, where people split into pro- and anti-change groups. Yet the two-sidedness is almost always a convenient fiction that promotes a war story plot structure, often resulting in groups demonizing one another.

Yet, as Allen points out, environmental systems are richly diverse, with various perspectives interpreting what is happening, contributing their skills and points of view, and receiving from the system in many ways. Helping people notice and understand these many more points of view can help a group move beyond a two-sided contest of wills into recognizing greater complexity. Instead of fighting as a way of resolving conflict, we can then all become detectives. The natural task becomes sorting out the abundance of perspectives into some coherent pattern, as Sherlock Holmes would do with "who done it" clues. Only our detective work would be involved in weaving together story lines that figure out, "What is the issue?" "What relationships are involved in it?" and "What can we do to realize the best possible outcome?"

My hope for this book is that it will become a widely read and shared manual for thinking in a twenty-first century way—one ideal for teams and groups faced with complex problems. Ideally group members would read the book, discuss it with one another, and then make these lessons part of their everyday decision-making and long-term planning. Short of that, it is an easy and fun read that I believe can provide any reader with a new and valuable lens for sorting out ways to assist families, friendship groups, work teams, or any social system at all.

—Carol S. Pearson, Ph.D., D.Min.
Author and Editor of *The Transforming Leader:*
New Approaches to Leadership for the 21st Century

Introduction

In northeast India, there is a state called Meghalaya, the *abode of the clouds*. It is a densely forested beautiful mountainous terrain. It is also the wettest place on earth, receiving over 470 inches of rain each year. Most of the rain falls in the monsoon season, which can cause the streams and rivers to turn into raging torrents of water. This region of India is known for its living bridges[1], a beautiful complex network of roots that are trained to form bridges made from living trees. People native to this region have found a way to tap nature's abundance to build a network of bridges strong enough to withstand the turbulent waters when streams increase in size and volume during the rainy season.

The strangler fig tree has a tangled root system that holds it to river banks. It also produces dangling roots from its branches. The native people plant these fig trees on one side of a stream bank and train their roots to grow across the water to anchor to a bank on the other side. Over the course of two human lifetimes, the original tree and its roots are nurtured and directed to create a beautiful

1 https://www.youtube.com/watch?v=KD_iidGaWcI

living bridge. As these bridges grow they become strong resilient structures that can last over 500 years—a living architecture.

Ever since I first heard of these remarkable bridges, they have shaped and expanded my thinking and my work in leadership and organizations. For instance, the living bridges have given me insights into how to view leadership transition. Instead of approaching the transition between a retiring executive and a new leader as an abrupt ending and new beginning, I now seek to imagine how the organization can create a living bridge where the knowledge and wisdom of the retiring executive remains in the organization and the new leader extends that legacy into the future for multiple generations of leadership. The idea of an organizational living bridge helps me to think about the tangible and intangible elements to be sustained in a seamless transition of leadership.

The living bridges of Meghalaya serve as a beautiful and fitting metaphor for this book, *Leading from the Roots: Nature Inspired Leadership Lessons for Today's World*. Like the strangler fig, the book anchors itself in nature and scales nature's design principles and the dynamics of living systems across to organizational leadership.

Metaphors and Mindsets:

I have come to understand that our thinking and actions are shaped by our worldviews and the metaphors we use to comprehend and describe how the world works. I believe that we each have mindsets, much deeper than our job descriptions, that inform how we approach responsibilities and challenges in our work and our lives. My focus has always been developmental. In my work in and with organizations, I have always seen leadership through a developmental lens and have tried to lead in a way that enhances the individual and professional development of the people I work with and supervise.

When I became a vice president, I started to see how the organization itself can create conditions conducive to developing employees. I began to see how organizational processes like performance review weren't just about evaluation and accountability. They were also opportunities to provide feedback that could help that individual grow as a professional and as a person. As a consultant for the past eighteen years, I have applied this developmental point of view to my work with individuals as an executive coach and to my work with organizations helping them to generate and support more effective, innovative, and healthy cultures.

Some organizations I have worked for have been better than others, some have been exhilarating, others challenging, and still others have been filled with painful lessons. Some organizations have made me a better person and professional while I worked in them. Through the years, I noticed how these organizations were designed and led differently than the dysfunctional organizations I have worked for or with. I wondered, what made the difference? Was it possible for organizations to change, to improve, to evolve?

Through my work and my study of nature and biomimicry, I came to understand that organizations are not inert objects, as traditionally thought, but are living systems. Given that organizations are filled with human beings, it doesn't take a huge leap of faith to believe that a living system would emerge from all the life that shows up every day. And as living systems, organizations have the capacity to evolve.

The more I learned about the lessons and designs of natural systems, and saw what did and didn't work in organizations, the more I intentionally cultivated a living-systems mindset. When I internalize the dynamics of living systems and apply the design principles found in biomimicry, it changes everything about my consulting work and the subsequent results. I have found that working to grow generous organizations and systems allows change to occur faster, takes less energy and resources, and is more sustainable.

The premise of my work and this book is that our organizations are living systems that can evolve and grow to become more generous in how they organize themselves, and how they contribute back to our communities and the world. I turn to nature's design principles and living systems mindsets for lessons on how to grow generous organizations—complex, diverse, self-sustaining, and highly resilient—and explore what kind of leadership could help us accomplish this.

Leading with a Living System Mindset:

In leadership, applying design thinking is about finding powerful questions that help us think and act differently. The following questions help to shift the focus of leadership from a traditional worldview to what leaders would focus on in a living system. Throughout the book, I grapple with these questions, offering insights from nature and examples from my work with organizations.

What can I unleash?

Traditionally positional leaders and managers assumed that their organizational environment was predictable and controllable. Their organizing question was, "What can I control to create the best outcome?" Strategic planning is a good example of this. Strategic plans are based on what we think will leverage the future of the organization. They are typically framed in a linear plan with a three-year timeframe. We assign names of people responsible for the objectives or activities in the plan and hold them accountable to achieve the desirable result. This approach triggers supervisory meetings to ensure things are getting done.

But in a living system, things are complex, dynamic, and unpredictable. So the question becomes, "What can I unleash" and flows from this different worldview. It refers to the untapped and even unknown tangible and intangible energies in the organization. Shifting the focus even further to, "What can I unleash in service of the higher purpose of the organization?" allows for the untapped energies and talents to come forward to help advance the work of the organization.

What interactions will make this work?

Traditionally positional leaders and managers have a worldview that assumes a closed system where control is possible, everything is separate and discrete, and each effort needs a person to drive the project. Therefore, their focus is on who is going to get the job done and the default assumption is that they need to find a person in authority to lead this effort.

In a living system, everything is connected. Because things are connected and dynamic, the focus of leaders shifts from assigning someone to lead the project to designing interactions that will accomplish the desired goal. As leaders, we need to be asking: "What talent and knowledge needs to be in the room? How do we bring together the right people to help accomplish this task? How do we sequence interactions to gain momentum for this project?"

How do we welcome resistance?

Traditionally organizations work to avoid resistance. The assumption is that resistance hurts the organization because it creates conflict, which in turn, hinders productivity. Therefore, resistance needs to be eliminated, overcome, or shut down.

In a living system, we assume that diversity of perspectives and opinions enhances the quality of decision-making and understanding. Thus, tensions are normal, and opposition is necessary for understanding and achieving wholeness. Therefore, resistance needs to be welcomed.

How do we influence the field or our organization's culture?

Traditionally we build and maintain organizational structures and processes that control individual behavior and keep the organization in a stable and predictable state. This flows from the assumption that things are simple and static, and it is not necessary to change the larger culture or field. Therefore, if leaders control individual behavior the organization will be stable as well.

In a living system, things are complex, mutually shaping, and dynamic. Given this, we need to acknowledge that an organization that is constantly learning and evolving is more adaptive to changes in the external environment—and thus is actually more stable. It isn't effective or efficient or even possible, to build an adaptive organization by controlling individual behaviors or attitudes. But because organizations are complex connected systems, when we influence the culture, it will in turn influence individuals. Therefore, leaders of living systems strive to influence the field or organization's culture by being open to the external environment and adaptive changes.

> *How can we transform energy? How do we use the energy*
> *of the larger system to help design sustainable change?*

Traditionally, a leader's change strategy was to come up with a vision and then drive change down through the organization and allocate resources and attention to insure the change stays in place. This approach flows from the assumption that organizations are static and require energy to shift the status quo and that change must come from the top.

Thinking of change as transforming energy flows from the assumption that things are dynamic and that every organization has energy that is not currently tapped or that is wasted on processes or structures that don't help the organization achieve its highest potential. It also assumes that there is local expertise and self-organizing capabilities throughout the organization; change does not have to come from or be managed from the top. In a living system, we look to design change that once accomplished, the resources allocated (time, attention, money etc.) can be released to support another adaptive cycle.

Leading from the Roots: Nature Inspired Leadership Lessons for Today's World is written for people who are seeking another way to lead and work in organizations. I believe there are many practitioners who are experimenting and seeking to create healthier and more effective teams, departments, and organizations. We have the power and possibility to create generous organizations where the people in them and the larger organization thrive in relationship to the community and world in which it is placed. The hope of this book is to give language and a way to articulate design principles for practitioners who are already leading this way in their organizations. For others, it will provide a vision of what we can become as well as innovative ways of thinking and acting that aligns with the dynamics of living systems and uses lessons from nature as inspiration.

> *Leaders can help their organizations grow into generous organizations.*
> *This book tells you how.*

Three Frameworks to Leading from the Roots:

This book uses three key frameworks to help us imagine how we can help to grow organizations that are healthy and productive places that work for all.

The first framework is that organizations can evolve. Currently most of our organizations are consumptive in nature. They are designed and led in ways that consume more resources than they produce. If we define consumption in a broader way, we can see how these consumptive organizations devour not only raw materials but also the resources of their employees and customers, and that they give little back in return. Some organizations have evolved to where their relationships are more reciprocal; they focus on life-giving interactions and are more self-sustaining, resilient and generous. These generous organizations are often found in sectors where there is a great deal of external turbulence and extraordinary talent is sought to maintain the adaptive capacity and resilience of the organization. The evolution from consumptive to generous can make an organization a better and more attractive place for people to work and at the same time be more innovative, adaptive, and productive. This book is a road map to helping organizations evolve toward a generous system.

The second framework is that nature has lessons to inspire and help us to think differently about our leadership and our organizations. Nature has simple short-lived ecologies and resilient long-term mature ecologies. There are significant differences in how they are designed and structured. Type I and Type II ecologies primarily depend on the nutrients in the soil to give them life. These consumptive ecologies consume nutrients without giving anything back into the system, depleting resources, and as a result are not designed to be resilient over time. Type III mature ecologies, are considered generous systems because they exchange nutrients with other species in diverse environments. This enables all the species to thrive without depending solely on the nutrients from the soil—creating a more complex, resilient and generous system. This book uses the underlying designs of the generous systems found in old growth forests, mature prairies, and mature coral reefs as a model, muse, and lens to rethink leadership practices and organizational design.

The third framework is that working with the dynamics of living systems enable us to lead in ways that are more effective for the complex challenges we face today. We developed our traditional leadership theories and practices at a time when we viewed organizations as machine-like and our organizations were largely closed systems. While there were issues, they were somewhat contained and so problems were easily understood and addressed. We would analyze all the parts and see what was not working, fix it, and reassemble the system. But today, our organizations are open systems and as such there are always new variables to consider. Using the old models, we create problems and dysfunction, and waste time and energy. Since we can't solve complex problems in the traditional way, we need to *design our way* out of our challenges. This is a fundamental shift in the way we approach problems. It calls for a higher level of creativity and innovation. To solve complex problems, we must go up to the balcony and look at the patterns that are occurring, taking in all the new and constantly changing variables.

This book is the result of years of applying these frameworks and lessons from nature to create a new, more ecological way of leading. It is designed to help leaders understand and articulate how living systems inspire powerful and lasting development of the organizations and communities we care about.

Chapter One: Living Systems, Generous Organizations introduces the concepts of consumptive and generous organizations, nature's design principles for generous systems, and the dynamics of living systems that need to be understood to help us shift our leadership.

The following eight chapters each explore a particular design principle from nature and how they can inspire us to think differently about leadership and create generous organizations.

- *Chapter Two: Nature Runs on Sunlight*
- *Chapter Three: In Nature Waste Is Never Wasted*
- *Chapter Four: Nature Fits Form to Function*
- *Chapter Five: Nature Rewards Cooperation*
- *Chapter Six: Nature Banks on Diversity*
- *Chapter Seven: Nature Curbs Excess from Within*
- *Chapter Eight: Nature Depends on Local Expertise and Self-Organization*
- *Chapter Nine: Nature Taps the Power of Limits*

In *Chapter Ten: Leading from a Living Systems Mindset,* we will examine how leadership mindsets, behavior, and outcomes change when they are aligned with the dynamics of living systems. In this chapter, I offer examples of how I have used the living systems mindset in my work and how this has led to more creative, innovative and generous organizations.

Finally, *Chapter Eleven: Growing Generous Organizations* is a call to action for people interested in helping their organizations to evolve to be more diverse, self-sustaining, productive and resilient—to be generous organizations. It also explores critical (individual and organizational) developmental capacities that are essential for an organization to become a generous system.

Earlier this year I bought a book titled *This Idea Must Die: Scientific Theories That Are Blocking Progress* edited by John Brockman (2015). I love this title because it captures the essence of what it takes to build a leadership practice that grows a generous organization. It isn't just about what you add, it also requires an intentional letting go of previously held, unhelpful assumptions we hold about leadership, organizations, and people. In my yoga practice, there is a mindfulness question: What do we need to relinquish and what do we need to practice moving forward?

This letting go is necessary to developing innovative ways of thinking and working. Often when we learn new things we just add them to everything else we already know. We rarely take our old ideas out with the trash. These defaults reappear and cause our behavior to follow outdated lines and be incompatible with our current thinking. Often this makes us unable to find the answers we need, or as Albert Einstein said, "We cannot solve our problems with the same thinking we used when we created them." The art of letting go of old ideas, practices, and behaviors is part of the journey to growing and leading a generous organization. Learning from nature requires that we take on new areas of focus and ways of acting, recognizing how they may be different from traditional thinking and leadership behavior.

Therefore, throughout the book, I identify the new areas we need to focus on as well as the mindsets and behaviors that need to be intentionally released. I also conclude each chapter with a "Questions to Consider" section that raises issues and questions for you and your teams to consider as you incorporate these lessons from nature.

My hopes for this book are to help people reimagine what an organization can become. Some of us may have given up expecting organizations to be wonderful places to work or places where benefits and burdens are widely shared. Much less a place where there is a sense of larger purpose that brings meaning to our work. I want to invite us to raise our aspirations of what we should expect of our organizations and how they treat employees, customers, and other stakeholders. And finally, help us design our way out of systemic dysfunction and drama.

> *We can't solve complex organizational problems by breaking them down into parts, but we can design our way out of them using the inspiration that is found in nature.*

We know all these things are possible, because some organizations have already evolved to become generous. This book is written for people who want to accelerate this shift toward generous organizations in their workplaces.

CHAPTER ONE

Living Systems, Generous Organizations

Shifting From a Mechanistic To a Biological Worldview

During the twentieth century, we fell in love with the power of the machine. We saw how inventions like the automobile, airplane, computer, robot, and smart phone extended the reach of human beings in profound ways. Modern organizations came into being during the industrial revolution. We took the engineering designs we developed to create machines as models for organizational structures and functions. This machine-thinking even guided how we understood success, how we saw ourselves and treated others, and how we defined what leadership meant. While powerful, this view of the world has left us with enormous social and environmental damage, debts, and dismay. We need a new vision of leadership and organizations that once again extends the reach of human beings, but in very different ways and to very different ends.

Such a shift is underway. The twenty-first century is the Century of Biology (Brown, 2008). Just as the twentieth century looked to machines, the twenty-first century is looking to biology to inform how we think, organize, design, and lead our organizations. More and more, we are turning to nature as our mentor, model, and muse to inform the way we understand organizations and leadership and our aspirations for what our organizations can become. This changes everything.

With this new mindset, the emphasis on replication and uniformity is giving way to valuing and leveraging the uniqueness of culture and context. Instead of mass production, we have mass customization. Where we used to see organizations as objects and the people in them as objects or even as property of the organization, today we see organizations as living, complex, and interdependent systems just as in the natural world. Where we used to not think twice about using tremendous energy to extract value from all types of resources—natural, human and intellectual—now we are looking for ways to leverage our resources in gentler, non-toxic, self-replenishing ways.

When we realize our organizations are living systems rather than inert machines, it becomes clear why many of the traditional ways of leading and organizing don't work. Focusing on making a profit or holding onto power, sets the bar too low and ignores the reality of our interdependent world where connections and actions ripple across systems and create intentional and unintentional consequences. Our traditional way of leading and thinking about organizations has created systemic dysfunction, drama, and trauma in our workplaces. It has led to organizations that are based on consumption—consuming resources, people, and investments—giving little in return and in the long run are unsustainable.

We need a new way of leading that creates organizations that are generous and sustaining, and as such are healthier for the people who work in them, our communities and the planet. Our organizations need to evolve, and our worldview of leadership and its purpose needs to expand.

Organizations Can Evolve:

If we think of organizations as machine-like, then we probably assume we can improve them by reengineering them, but we are unlikely to believe that they evolve. But if we hold that organizations are living systems, then we can assume that organizations can and do, and even should, evolve. And that if these living systems do not evolve, if they do not progress, they may wither and die. We all have seen examples of this with organizations that have lost their purpose, have not stayed current with the marketplace, have consumed all their resources (natural, human, financial), or have been so dysfunctional that they dissolve or fall apart.

Ecosystem Attributes		
Stage I	Stage II	Stage III
·Emphasis on seeds: rapid growth ·High energy consumption, low nutrient conservation ·Few species, little symbiosis' ·Opportunistic consumption of plentiful resources	·Emphasis on roots and stems: structures that can last ·More balanced energy consumption and nutrient preservation ·More species ·More patient consumption	·Emphasis on self-renewal across generations ·Creates more nutrients than consumed: a "generous system" ·Web-like diversity ·Optimal resilience through complex, synergistic relationships
Example: weeds in a newly-plowed field	Example: perennial shrubs and woody seedlings	Example: mature forest or prairie

Fortunately, we can draw inspiration and lessons for our organizations from Nature's 3.8 billion years of evolution and thousands of diverse living systems. It has used that time to create Type I, Type II and Type III ecologies, each of which has their counterpart in human organizations.

Type I ecologies are like weeds and annuals. They consume all their nutrients from the soil and don't contribute anything back. As a result, they are short-lived and not resilient. Organizations that are like Type I ecologies are consumptive. Startup ventures are comparable to Type I ecologies. These organizations consume their nutrients from the venture capital investments that fund them. They take resources to live, but don't give back to the bottom line. They only continue to live if conditions are favorable. When winter comes (or money runs out), they die.

Type II ecologies are also consumptive. These ecologies are composed of perennials, small shrubs, and short-lived trees. They consume most of their nutrients from the soil and give little back, but they live longer than weeds and annuals because they start to store nutrients for their own use in their roots, tubers, and bulbs. But they still consume more than they contribute.

Organizations that are like Type II ecologies are also consumptive. I like to think of these plants as comparable to organizational silos. In these organizations, departments are separated into silos where they spend much of their energy on their own needs and compete against one another for resources. Organizations at this level of evolution create and sell products to contribute to the organizational resources. They consume more resources than they contribute back to the world. There is a lot of waste to these organizations but sometimes it is hard for us to notice as this is considered normal organizational behavior.

Type III ecologies are complex diverse ecologies such as old growth forests or mature prairies. In these systems, the diverse plant and animal life develop mutually-beneficial relationships that provide nutrients to each other and give nutrients back to the soil. The plant and animal life contribute more to the ecosystem than they use, so life thrives. They are adaptive, self-sustaining, highly resilient and based on generosity. Type III ecologies and analogous organizations are generous systems. Generous organizations are highly productive, innovative, and continually adapt to be resilient—just as in nature. Generous organizations are multi-dimensionally diverse, complex, and interdependent. They welcome the tensions that help them continually adapt and maintain a dynamic equilibrium.

Luckily, we don't have to create generous organizations out of thin air. We already have examples of these kinds of organizations in operation today. We all have experienced or know someone who works in a great organization. At conferences, we hear people say, I love my job or I love my organization. These people know what a generous organization feels like—open, affirming, innovative— and how it motivates them to engage and contribute at their highest levels of excellence.

> *How do we transform our consumptive organizations*
> *to become generous organizations?*

Today, we have many examples of evolving organizations. Many start-ups (Type I ecologies) are beginning to develop staff, business plans, shared purpose and visions to create more sustainable and generous organizations. Other organizations are moving away from protected silos (Type II ecologies) towards integrated relationships. In these organizations, leadership teams are showing up to serve the entire organization, not just their department. Organizations are becoming more aware of the risks associated with homogeneity, for instance some firms are working to create gender and racial parity. Investment firms are tracking these movement and using diversity, social responsibility, and environmental-friendly standards as investment strategies knowing that on average these organizations give back better returns over time. All these actions suggest organizations are evolving from being consumptive to something else. I suggest that the next level of organizational evolution will be toward the generous systems found in Type III ecologies in nature.

I have titled this book *Leading from the Roots: Nature Inspired Leadership Lessons for Today's World* because I believe this is the direction that leadership needs to move toward. In an interdependent world, we need a higher purpose that spans the boundaries of our organizations, sectors, and geographies, and creates conditions conducive to the life of our organizations, our communities and our planet. And what better teacher and muse can we look toward than Nature, with its 3.8-billion-year research and development experience?

In the next section, I explore the dynamics found in living systems. Leaders can use nature's design principles (described in Chapters Two through Nine) paired with these living-system dynamics to shift their leadership practices to grow generous organizations.

Design Lessons Found In Nature:

> *What would leadership look like if its highest purpose was
> to ensure that future generations thrived?*

In 2002, Janine Benyus wrote a book titled *Biomimicry: Innovation Inspired by Nature*. Biomimicry seeks sustainable solutions drawing on nature's time-tested patterns and strategies. When I read the book, I felt the content was profound and it sparked a journey of experimentation on how I could apply biomimicry design principles to the living organizations that I was working with. While the field of biomimicry continues to evolve in its thinking of nature's design (Baumeister, 2014), I have found that Benyus' original principles raise valuable lines of inquiry for us to follow as we build a robust living bridge from nature to organizations and leadership.

In this book, I use both biomimicry and nature as a source of lessons and design principles to lead in a more effective, efficient, and innately satisfying way, and to provide a vision of leadership that can foster genuine, transformational change. I have made slight changes in the wording to reflect what I've learned in applying these to my work with organizations.

- *Chapter Two: Nature Runs on Sunlight*
- *Chapter Three: In Nature Waste Is Never Wasted*
- *Chapter Four: Nature Fits Form to Function*
- *Chapter Five: Nature Rewards Cooperation*
- *Chapter Six: Nature Banks on Diversity*
- *Chapter Seven: Nature Uses Feedback to Curb Excess*
- *Chapter Eight: Nature Depends on Local Expertise
  and Self-Organization*
- *Chapter Nine: Nature Taps the Power of Limits*

As we shift our leadership practice to incorporate these design principles, our organizations will begin to evolve towards a generous system.

Understanding the Dynamics of Living Systems:

To apply nature's design principles and move from a mechanistic to a biological way of leading, we need to rethink our basic assumptions about how the world works. We will need to understand and work with organizations as living systems (Allen, 2015).[2] The following are the seven lessons I have learned that explain the dynamics and the forces at play in living systems. Together, they help to describe the predominant conditions one finds when operating in complex, living systems. You can imagine them like Russian nesting dolls, where each concept narrows successively from the first big idea of "interdependence" to the final, most immediate concept of "this moment."

1. *Living systems are interdependent—change in one part of the system influences other parts of the system in expected and unexpected ways.*

Nature is interdependent. Everything mutually creates everything else, there are no independent entities. John Muir (1911) captured this aspect of nature when he said, "When we try to pick out anything by itself, we find it hitched to everything else in the Universe" (p.110). Everything we do affects the world in both observable and unpredictable ways. Similarly, what we perceive as external is central to our very being. Assuming interdependence presents a radical challenge to how many of us perceive things: I'm a self-made man! I think; therefore I am! That is not my responsibility! But I would challenge anyone to actually disprove the basic assumption of interdependence.

Unfortunately, most of us have not yet internalized our place within an interdependent context (Hutchins, 2014). We are drawn to separation of function and division of labor in the name of efficiency. Our logic models are linear and reflect a single cause and effect. If we do "A" then "B" will happen and that creates "C." I used to be a math major and loved these logic trails. However, I now see organizations as complex overlapping spider webs where the links and relationships are diverse and vary in strength. When a fly gets stuck in a spider web, the fly tries to get free. In so doing, it creates ripples in the web (Allen & Cherrey, 2000). Changes that occur far away can create disturbances locally. These intended and unintended consequences are hard to predict in a system and therefore, linear logic is no longer helpful.

[2] Leading Living Systems. TEDX talk https://www.youtube.com/watch?v=DAwHiM-1FnM)

Interdependent systems also ask us to change our strategies to accomplish goals and tasks. For example, if we assume things are independent, it is natural to ask, "Who can make this work?" Or "who can get this done?" But if we assume things are interdependent, the question becomes "What interactions will make this work?" It may be that when we shine a light on interdependence, we can help others to understand how relationships and emotions in human living systems work.

2. *Living systems become more diverse as they evolve.*

As living systems grow and evolve, they become more diverse. If we use the human body as an example of a living system, we are clearly more complex and diverse than the single cell organisms that our life started with. For example, we have muscular, nervous, circulatory, endocrine, lymphatic, digestive, respiratory, urinary, reproductive, integumentary, and skeletal systems that all provide critical and distinct functions within our body. We carry both diversity and interdependence in our body, most of which function together without conscious thought. This diversity of functions is designed to operate interdependently with other aspects of our body.

Our organizations are filled with diversity of perspectives, viewing points, functions, ages, ethnicities, genders, experiences, talents, and gifts. When we see our organizations as a living system, we need to see this diversity as a natural phenomenon within our organizations. We can then ask, "How do we leverage diversity to help our organization evolve into a generous system?"

3. *Living systems are never static, they are always in flux.*

Once we begin internalizing the notion of interdependence, it's important to know that everything we're connected to is always changing. This, of course, means we are as well. The prevailing wisdom is that people don't like change. This may be true, but change is a fundamental characteristic of being.

Our aversion to change skews the way we understand leadership. Too often, leadership is imagined as an external power source needed to start the (dreaded) change process, like a key starting a motor. This is sometimes called "change management." But when we see that change is a natural state, we begin to rethink how we approach the role of leadership.

I have a colleague who used to be a buyer for a major retail chain. She has a refreshing view of change because her experience in retail was that fashion changed all the time. When she became a leadership consultant, she was inclined to see change as a natural event in organizational life. This gave her a special insight with her clients because she could help them relate to how the changes in their work were akin to fashion's ongoing transformation. Change is not something to be fought and we do not have to initiate it. Instead, we need to consider how change is already occurring and what direction it is moving in. The leadership question is not, "How can I create change?" it is, "How do I transform the energy that already exists in the living system into life-supporting change?"

4. *Living systems are filled with feedback loops that facilitate evolution.*

In an interdependent system, we can sense the direction of change through feedback loops. Nature is filled with feedback loops that reinforce certain behaviors and other feedback loops that balance the system by discouraging behavior. This is how the living system thrives over time.

In my consulting practice, I use feedback to facilitate intentional change. Through qualitative interviews, I am able to find unexpressed or partially expressed themes and patterns in the thoughts of people in an organization.

When I present my findings to the interviewees, it creates a new feedback loop. The data I report often raises issues that haven't been acknowledged by the full group, but have been felt individually and expressed in cliques. By naming these issues, the feedback can unleash a powerful force that drives the entire organization to become more effective. While this technique is similar to what other organizational development practitioners might do, intentionally using feedback as a way to help the team or organization evolve increases the power of this intervention.

5. *Living systems cannot be steered or controlled, only attracted or nudged.*

Being interdependent and connected by feedback loops means that behaviors are mutually-reinforcing and create strong redundancies. One result of this is that networks inherently resist control. Human beings can be attracted or nudged to change, but when they are pushed or forced, they resist. Adults like to be asked for their opinion. They like the opportunity to freely share their talents to help make something meaningful happen, rather than being told to do so. One would think this would be obvious to leaders, but I think many are deeply attached to a top-down assumption of leadership. It blinds them to the fact that trying to "drive" change takes more time, money, and resources than leveraging the natural tendencies of the living system.

6. *Living systems only accept solutions that the system helps to create.*

When the living system and the people in it are actively engaged in co-creating change, there isn't a reason to resist change. We can take this a step further and say that, as in all living systems, people support what they help to create. This is obvious; the homeowner-built deck is swept regularly and re-stained on schedule, whereas the one at the hotel is treated ambivalently. In the same way, a vision and values statement created solely by a management team ends up in the employee's recycling bin. But the one that is articulated through a genuine, participatory employee engagement process is posted by staff and referenced during moments of contention: "That idea isn't who we are—but THIS is!"

I once worked with an organization which was recovering from a toxic leader. The new CEO wanted to shift towards a healthier culture. He noticed the staff's need to heal and asked me to facilitate a retreat to help with that process. At the end of the retreat, they came up with some recommendations to continue the move toward a healthy culture. They decided to generate a working group to develop operating principles for all staff members. These operating principles spoke to their communications, relationships, and how they treated each other. It became a living document in the organization that reshaped their behavior. If you've never experienced that level of employee ownership, you may regard the idea with understandable skepticism. But such moments of authentic interactions do happen and can result in widely-supported decisions.

7. *Living systems only pay attention to what is meaningful to
    them here and now.*

This final dynamic firmly ties the experience within an interdependent system to our everyday concrete moments. During our every waking hour, we give attention to something. It may be a loved one, a meal, a task, a phone call, or even staring out the window without purpose. Whatever it is, and despite what apologists of multi-tasking might think, we can give our conscious attention to only one thing at a time in a single moment. This helps explain why living systems only pay attention to what they care about. That might sound obvious, but it is often neglected by leaders who have not fostered feedback loops to help them better understand the changes occurring in the system they are part of (not apart from). This can cause leaders to force changes because they do not know how to communicate why what they say matters to others.

Leaders often don't appreciate how meaningless information can be if it falls outside a person's sphere of concern. They tell employees that a change is happening and how the change will occur, but fall short of explaining the change in terms of why it matters to the employees. The result can be confusing and frustrating. In a living system, we need to articulate why things matter. If we want employees to actively support the larger purpose of the organization, we need to answer these questions:

*   *Why does this matter to the individual employee?*
*   *Why does this matter to the organization?*
*   *Why does this matter to the larger society?*

In Summary:

Organizations were created as a part of the industrial revolution and shaped by our fascination with machines. When positional leaders hold the conscious or unconscious assumption that organizations are machine-like, they see them as separate and inert, rather than as interdependent living systems. This mindset leads to consumptive organizations that devour resources and give little in return, and are ultimately unsustainable. We need an organizational vision that recognizes organizations as living systems that can evolve and be led to be more generous. Nature provides us with many examples of generous living systems that are diverse, complex, self-sustaining and resilient. By using nature as an inspiration and model, leaders can begin to create generous organizations that work for all. Unlike the consumptive organization, generous organizations use fewer resources, are more effective, and are more fun to work in!

Questions to Consider:

This book rests on the question: Can organizations evolve and if so, toward what end? If we see our organizations as living systems, we can begin to help our organizations shift to be more generous ones. Here are a few questions that leadership teams can reflect on to begin this process.

- *Do we believe that our organization is a living system?*
- *Do we believe that our organization can and is evolving?*
- *Where do we see our organization along a continuum between highly consumptive (Type I ecology of weeds and annuals) to somewhat consumptive (Type II perennials and weeks) and highly generous (Type III ecology, cooperative, diverse and highly resilient)?*
- *What are the indicators that exist in our organization that suggests that we are leading a living system?*
- *What organizational behaviors do not align with living system dynamics?*
- *If we are migrating towards a generous organization, what are the indicators that support that shift?*

CHAPTER TWO

Nature Runs on Sunlight

Nature runs on generosity. All living beings—plant life, birds, reptiles and mammals—are powered by the energy from the sun. Sunlight is not only ubiquitous, it is free! The sun's energy is so abundant and reliable, such a constant feature in our life, that we sometimes take it for granted. Its crucial contribution to life on this earth disappears from our consciousness. Having just experienced a solar eclipse of the sun, one imagines the fear the ancients must have felt when the moon blotted out the sun. Perhaps they had more of an appreciation of the importance of the life-giving feature of the sun than we modern humans do.

It is stunning to realize that all life starts with such a generous act. Further, it is paired with another generous feature of nature—photosynthesis. Sunlight only works as an energy source if it shines down on grass, trees, and other plant life. The sunlight that shines on the moon can't convert its energy into life because there aren't trees and grass to partner with. Photosynthesis is required to transform the sun's energy into myriad forms that support all life on Earth.

Bacteria, algae, and plants accept the sun's energy and make food in the form of their bodies which, in turn, feed other living beings (Callenbach, 1998). The sun's energy continues to support life through the relationships between the *primary producers* like grass, trees, algae and *primary consumers* that take the sun's converted energy and produce food for other animals, such as cows that eat grass and produce food like milk, cheese and meat that others consume. It is through these relationships that life thrives. Generosity is not only found in the sun's gift of energy but also in these mutually-beneficial exchanges in mature ecological systems.

What is an organization's version of sunlight?

Using nature as a muse leads me to wonder if there is a comparable generous indispensable energy source in our organizations that is largely invisible to us. Traditionally organizations have used land, capital and labor as primary resources to create products and maintain a competitive advantage. More recently, we have added intellectual capital to the mix. But what if there is another powerful source of energy that exists naturally in our organizations; one that only shows itself under certain conditions—when the leadership and organization are designed to be generous instead of consumptive.

Traditionally we have thought of employees as disengaged labor or extensions of the organization that management needs to direct, oversee, and motivate to optimize production. However, we also have many examples of engaged teams that are infused with positive energy and achieve extraordinary results for their organizations (Lencioni, 2012). Experience tells us that when people bring their positive energy to the workplace remarkable things can happen. This energy is a valuable unquantified resource which many leaders overlook or neglect.

Recently, I did a cultural audit with an organization that had many talented people. However, the dominate emotion was of fear and scarcity. People felt that they needed to protect themselves from the whims of the organization. They didn't feel safe. This caused people to bring negative or neutral energy to their jobs. I saw my role as helping the organization and its culture shift from a consumptive organization based in scarcity and fear to a generous one that is hopeful and confident about its future. To do that, we needed to see if we could shift the polarity of energy from negative to positive. Relationships are powerful conduits because our universe is built on comprehensive interdependence and our human connections reflect this reality (Capra, 1996; Wheatley, 1992). The quality of our relationships impacts the nature, flow, and polarity of the human energy we release at work (Allen & Mease, 2002). When the quality of the relationships between co-workers is good, positive energy is exchanged. But when the relationships with colleagues are strained, anchored in distrust or fear, our energy is used for self-protection and not available to the larger organization.

Positive energy is the ubiquitous asset in a generous organization (Quinn, 2015). When positive energy is present, we look forward to coming to work and being part of a team where we feel connected. Our leadership practices can intentionally nurture positive energy. When our teams and organizations recognize and facilitate interdependence, we can increase the positive flow of human energy. A high-performance team is a simple example of this principle. They work in an interdependent way and the positive energy becomes another team asset that enhances their effectiveness and performance. Anyone who has worked in a wonderful team is familiar with the positive energy that flows through the relationships on the team.

What would happen if we saw positive human energy as a large-scale resource equal to intellectual capital or other natural resources? Would it change how we think about our employees? Would it change the way we lead people? Would it change how we work together?

Organizational photosynthesis:

If people and their energy are an essential resource in our organizations, what are the conditions and steps that can "photosynthesize" this human "sunlight" into positive, life-giving energy? People are different from nature in that they have consciousness. We can choose to bring positive, neutral, or negative energy to our workplaces and our work. What actions, relationships, or processes can translate human energy into authentic, critically-aware positivity?

When I do culture audits for organizations, two of my favorite questions to ask are: What drains your energy at work? What generates positive energy for you at work? Over the years, consistent themes and patterns have emerged from these interviews. Personal conflicts, tensions in relationships, meaningless work, uncooperative colleagues, difficult challenges with clients or customers, and not being valued are the most frequent answers for what drains energy. The most common answers for what generates positive energy includes great colleagues, a cooperative workplace, meaningful work that matters, a feeling that your talents are utilized and respected, and having fun while the work gets done.

I can't imagine that these answers surprise anyone. There is proof all around us. When my consulting clients have more positive energy their workplaces are highly productive and innovative. When negative energy pervades, productivity is reduced as employees' energy is drained by dysfunction, distrust and self-protection. Even so, I am stunned that many of my clients don't see positive energy as a diagnostic for the health of their organization.

If we recognize people and their energy as a significant organizational resource, what is the "photosynthesis" or process that would turn this resource into a life-giving source of support? Drawing on my consulting experience, I have found that three powerful practices unleash positive human energy at work: authentic relationships, shared higher purpose and reciprocity.

Authentic relationships:

Positive energy is increased in an organization when people bring their authentic selves to work. Yet most organizations are structured on hierarchies which put the manager in a position of having *power over* the employees (Brown, 1986). This causes the employees to feel like their relationship with their supervisor isn't based in authenticity rather that the manager has an agenda and he wants his employees to deliver the results. This often leads employees to try and please their supervisor which is not necessarily an authentic expression of who they are. The effect of their inauthentic relationship is that neither the manager nor the employees feel free to bring their positive energy to their work. It is always muted by the *power over* nature of the relationship.

Yet there are leaders and managers that work to transcend this *power over* relationship and seek to treat their employees as individuals that bring unique value to the organization. There are many high-performing teams that are based in this more authentic relationship and the amount of positive human energy can be felt in the team and seen in the results (Lencioni, 2012; Quinn, 2015).

For example, there is a large privately-held multinational business that regularly does engagement surveys. Recently their results showed very high engagement in 55% of the company. In each of the departments with high engagement scores, there was a high correlation to superior results and performance. In these departments, teams, and divisions, the quality of leadership made a difference in the results. These employees said their supervisor saw them as unique individuals and they felt highly valued for their contributions. The organization's notable results confirm the value of positive human energy as an organizational asset and shows that authentic relationships are a key aspect of "organizational photosynthesis."

Shared higher purpose:

There is an old story of a person watching three brick layers. He talks to the first brick layer and asks him what he is doing; he answers, "I am laying bricks." He goes to the next and asks him what he is doing, and this brick layer says, "I am building a wall." The observer then asks the third brick layer and his answer is startlingly different, he says, "I'm building a cathedral." This simple story has a lot to teach us about developing a shared higher purpose on our teams and in our organizations.

> *Would your employees say that they are laying bricks,*
> *building a wall or building a cathedral?*

Having a shared higher purpose is another key component of organizational photosynthesis that translates human energy into life-giving energy. Authentic connection to something greater than us unleashes positive human energy. In the twentieth century, we were enamored with efficiency and created assembly lines where people stood and focused on a narrow function (the equivalent of laying bricks) for hours and hours. While we have fewer people working on assembly lines these days, this organizational history still unconsciously shapes our job descriptions and expectations of employees. Breaking down jobs into such narrow functions works against the development of a shared higher purpose that would unleash positive human energy—an organization's version of a free generous resource.

For a shared higher purpose to be used as photosynthesis, the goal must transcend the organization's desire for growth or profits. Its purpose must be to serve a larger need in the world (Hock 2005; Quinn, 2015). High-functioning nonprofits have something to teach for-profits about the link between collectively working toward a higher goal (building a cathedral) and human energy. Many non-profits and private foundations are very good at articulating a higher shared purpose. They build positive human energy through their recruitment process by attracting people who are drawn to the higher purpose and want to help the organization achieve its mission.

For example, I work with a human services agency in Minnesota. They are working to build communities where people thrive. It is very clear to the employees of this agency that what they do matters to their participants (their word for clients). As soon as you walk into any of their facilities you can feel the positive energy of the employees.

Reciprocity:

The third form of organizational photosynthesis is reciprocity. Reciprocity is the practice of exchanging things with others for mutual benefit. When we have reciprocity, our actions communicate our respect for others. Reciprocity is also revealed in how we interact with the world, including the choices we make, the products we purchase, and how we give back to others. For example, when buying organic food, I'm supporting reciprocity with the Earth and what I put into my body. When buying fair-trade coffee, I'm supporting the reciprocity that the company has with the people throughout its production and supply line.

In organizations, reciprocity exists when teams and their members treat each other with equity and respect. In doing so, trust is built. Trust breaks down the defenses that hinder positive human energy, unleashing creativity and fostering generous mutual benefits (reciprocity). A lack of trust can lead to negative energy and can impact the entire culture of the organization

Recently a client discussed a problem he was having at work. A colleague in a collaborative working team was asked to be responsible for the project's budget. The team had a history of practicing reciprocity with each other and was an effective and productive team. However, when the colleague was given this responsibility, she shifted her behavior to a supervisory role. This shift wasn't something the organization had asked for; she did it on her own volition. She thought that if she was responsible for the budget, she had control and power over the others in the group. What had been an innovative and productive team began to exhibit a decrease of trust and an increase of relationship tension. While reciprocity had been the norm, people began to withhold their active support for the project because they didn't like the way they were treated. Now the members of the working team couldn't wait to finish the project to get out of the relationship with the budget coordinator. My client was mourning the loss of the reciprocity, fun, and productivity that once exemplified their work.

These three photosynthetic components: authentic relationships, shared higher purpose and reciprocity are interdependent in nature. All three must be present for the photosynthesis to work. When they are encouraged and manifested in our teams, departments, and divisions, our organizations have access to a huge intangible resource in the form of positive human energy. Generous organizations, as mature ecosystems, optimize this positive energy. These organizations recognize and treat people as unique individuals with special skills and talents which in turn make them want to contribute their strengths to the work. Understanding this, leaders in generous organizations intentionally unleash the positive energy and creativity of their employees. This is particularly important when an organization is going through changes, looking to adapt to a new situation, or striving for innovation.

How does nature's lesson to "run on sunlight" inspire us to think differently about leadership?

As leaders, we need to see and embrace the human energy of our employees as an essential resource for our living organization. We need to shift our leadership practices to strengthen authentic relationships, higher shared purpose, and reciprocity in our work environments. This section articulates what we need to focus on and to let go of to make this happen.

1. We need to encourage interconnections and interdependencies.

The earliest written record of a living bridge was in 1844. As I mentioned in the Introduction, the living bridges took two lifetimes to grow, so they had to have been in existence for quite some time before they were discovered by someone visiting the region. I like to imagine what the culture of the indigenous population was like in Meghalaya when the idea of a living bridge was first envisioned. The people had to see themselves as part of nature, living alongside and with their environment. They had to be able to see the beauty and utility of what was growing in their midst. It must have taken an unusual mind to visualize how the strangler fig's roots, freely growing without cultivation, could be used to cross streams when they turned into wild rivers during the monsoon season.

The people who first experimented with the living bridge design put their efforts into something they would never see in its final form and never benefit from. Their generous giving of their time and their commitment to serve future generations must have been informed by how they saw their relationships with each other and their community, and how they understood their interconnections and interdependencies with nature.

In our organizations, we are at the beginning of this journey.

We used to think of organizations as bounded, closed systems separate from the external environment. When we did consider the wider external environment, it was to develop strategies that protected our investments through closed-loop supply lines. However, we have plenty of evidence that shows us that our organizations are not closed, walled off entities. Rather they are open, living systems and there are many wild cards of unexpected shifts or challenges that show up daily from outside the system (Taleb, 2007). For instance, the U.S. stock market can have a good or difficult day depending on what is happening in Greece or China and sometimes the swings of fortune have very weak lines of causality. Some things are unexpected like the bird flu and its impact on turkey prices, while others may be driven by emotions or the political climate.

As leaders, we need to help our organizations, and the people within them, see the interdependent relationships we have with the external environment. We need to replace silo-thinking with a sense of how we are interconnected so we all can more accurately see the system and its dynamics. We need to focus on the nature of living systems and the implications that may have on the way we think and act.

For example, an organization I work with was revising its organizational chart. The organization wanted people to see their connections with each other, but the traditional organizational chart was better at showing how people were separated. They eventually experimented with an image of a tree, a living entity with a root system, trunk, many branches of varied sizes, and leaves. It was planted firmly in the soil and dependent on the outside resources of the sun, rain and climate to grow. This visual image helped people see that no matter what part of the tree their position occupied, they were still connected and needed by the whole. It also helped them see how they were firmly embedded in the outside environment and gave them greater clarity of the importance of that relationship. The image embodied a shared higher purpose, reciprocity and authentic relationships.

We need to let go of closed-systems assumptions. This flies in the face of human history where we have emphasized keeping control over our organizations. Yet control only works in closed systems where it is possible to minimize the number of variables that are in play. Thus we have worked hard to keep our systems closed. In fact, leadership and management literature has many books on how to manipulate things to maintain a closed system or help an organization be less vulnerable to changes in the external environment through controlling supply chains etc. Closed systems have a specific way of operating (Allen et. al. 1998). Decisions are made behind closed doors. Information flow is restricted to a need-to-know basis. Individuals tend to communicate with a restricted group of people with similar job titles. The culture of a closed system can silence, censor, or slow down feedback within the organization or from the external environment.

Those tactics seemed to work well in the first half of the twentieth century but by the early 2000s we were experiencing wild cards and black swans that totally disrupted a business model that had been in place for decades (Taleb, 2012). A living system is an open system. It can be influenced but not controlled. In a living system, closed-system processes have a cost to the sustainability of the whole. A living system needs rich and diverse feedback loops to evolve and adapt. Structures and functions need to be flexible and allow form to fit the function. The meaning behind a decision needs to be accessible and understood within the living system.

We need to let go of mindsets that view organizations as objects to be controlled. Most of our policies and procedures have been built on this twentieth century mindset. While this may have once suited the modes of production, as we move into the knowledge economy we need to adapt our organizational structures and processes. We are now beginning to understand that organizations are living systems that require a different set of leadership practices. One example of this change is seeing labor as talent, as opposed to property or cogs in a machine. This has created pressure on organizations to change their recruiting, development, and supervision of knowledge workers. It has also led to a growing focus on employees throughout their tenure, understanding that innovation and creativity comes from employees feeling valued and engaged in the work.

Advancements in technology have also tested our chain of command and dramatically reshaped communication. Through computers and mobile devices, we inadvertently created a networked culture that has supplanted the traditional hierarchical structure. Instead of having to go through an administrative assistant who guards the access to the C-suite, emails can now show up in anyone's inbox and anyone can invite people into the discussion by adding their names to the email and hitting the reply all. Technology has also allowed us to work from home challenging many rules and procedures, even the perception of what it means to be an employee.

Most of our human resource (HR) policies and processes are not designed for the fluid dynamics of living systems. For example, job descriptions are usually written with a list of specific duties or tasks that the individual is responsible for. This reinforces the mentality of the first brick layer who sees his job as only laying bricks. It dampens down positive human energy as it keeps people focused on tasks rather than the higher shared purpose thus limiting their potential, creativity, and innovation.

> *What would a job description look like if we started*
> *with a statement of our shared purpose?*

And instead of listing the duties, what if we articulated the outcomes that would be expected and how these were connected to the larger purpose? What if a job description articulated a philosophy of relationships and connections that this person would need to develop and maintain while doing their job? These shifts would give very different messages about the organization and the employee's relationship to the company.

One of the reasons it is important to focus on organizational culture and engagement is that our traditional HR policies have created exactly what we have in our organizations, a disengaged workforce that brings their negative or neutral energy to the workplace. Shifting to a living generous-systems perspective brings into question most, if not all, HR assumptions. Our systems of traditional supervision, leadership, strategic planning and dozens of other organizational processes need to be redesigned to align with the dynamics of living systems.

In my consulting practice, I work with many organizations that want to experiment with these processes to generate a positive and productive workplace. For example, in a community-based non-profit, we reframed the strategy by asking powerful questions with the entire staff instead of locking the organization into a specific set of initiatives. We included an annual generation of goals and objectives that related to the powerful strategic questions. These goals were adapted to what was going on in the external environment and were based on the organization's ongoing observations and learning. We also experimented with building the staff's capacity for ongoing scanning of the external environment, in order to perceive when outside changes were afoot that needed corresponding changes within the organization. (A more detailed description of this process is in Chapter Ten.)

2. We need to illuminate a shared higher purpose.

Leaders need to articulate their organization's shared higher purpose. It isn't enough to have a good bottom line. Higher purpose comes from the deep need that our organization is here to fulfill (Hock, 2005). It is the compelling reason for coming to work. Leaders need to name and remind staff what the higher purpose is and find ways to connect it with people's day-to-day work (Vaill, 1986). Helping people to connect their actions and behaviors to that larger shared purpose attunes them to this purpose, and it helps them make meaning of their work. This connection to meaningful work unleashes positive energy and purpose in the workplace. As people respond to and resonate with the purpose, they also actively see each other's role and function as sharing in that purpose. It reinforces how they see their relationships with others and reinforces reciprocity within the organization. By articulating this connection to the higher purpose and a sense of reciprocity, generous organizations reap the benefits of higher levels of positive energy.

When I worked in higher education, I saw my work as contributing to a better world. I knew that college graduates would disproportionally hold leadership and management positions. If I could help college students to become fully functioning adults who could manage their emotions and care about the broader world, they would take those qualities with them wherever they went and contribute accordingly. This clarity of meaning helped me see how my work mattered and shaped how I approached my work.

We need to let go of focusing on the parts instead of the whole. In closed systems, we solve problems by breaking them down and analyzing them (Snowden and Boone 2007). We find what is broken, and then repair or replace it. We do not look beyond the individual part. In living systems, the sum is always greater than the part, and we understand that we can't solve the problem by just focusing on the part. Instead we need to go up to the balcony and see the overall organization, the external environment, and how they interrelate. From this perspective, we can create a strategy based on our sense of patterns, our sense of the whole, and our higher shared purpose.

3. We need to create conditions conducive to authentic relationships in the workplace.

Another lesson to be taken from nature is how it creates conditions conducive to life (Benyus, 2002). The way nature does this is embedded in the deep design principles that shape life on this planet and supports its continued existence. Despite catastrophic disruption and the extinction of some species, life continues. The line from Jurassic Park "life finds a way" captures how nature is designed to support the conditions necessary for life.

> *What conditions would support authentic relationships in organizations?*

Intentionally shaping and supporting a positive and transparent organizational culture creates conditions conducive to authentic relationships. It is important to remember that what leaders model shapes the culture of the organization, especially what we do when the organization is in crisis. If we want to grow generous organizations, we should start by modeling authenticity in our relationships and expect others to do the same.

I once helped a senior leadership team do a team-based performance review. Their board was in the process of hiring a new CEO and the interim co-presidents needed to complete individual performance reviews of the senior team. The interim leaders didn't feel comfortable doing the reviews because they were colleagues before they were asked to step in as interim co-presidents and would return to being colleagues afterwards. The leadership team had developed a strong degree of trust and honesty with each other and wanted to see if it was possible to do a team-based performance review of each other. Every member of the leadership team agreed to participate in this process. As the group coach, I facilitated the process. Each member presented key successes and challenges they had faced in the last year, questions and clarifications were invited, and then each colleague gave specific feedback to the individual based on their experience over the past year. The experience challenged people to be open, honest, and direct with their colleagues. The process enabled them to raise questions, see challenges, and highlight strengths that might not have been considered in another format. In addition, by sharing these reviews, the team as a whole was able to advance its work with each other—being more aware of the pitfalls and possibilities of their work together. The process and outcome deepened their trust and authenticity of their relationships to the benefit of the team and the organization.

4. We need to recognize positive human energy as a measure of organizational health.

When the energy is off or turning negative, it is a sign that something significant is going on in the organization that is making it less healthy and productive. Therefore, as leaders, we need to focus on the quality and quantity of human energy that is being unleashed day to day in service of the higher shared purpose (Allen & Mease, 2002). When we see everyone as part of a living system, we become aware of how their issues can impact the energy that exists in our organization. People's fears, their ability to manage their emotions, and their ability to work for and care about a shared higher purpose all affect the energy of the organization.

But the reality is that people's worldviews impact their behavior. If they see the world through a lens of independence instead of interdependence, they will act accordingly. When they see the world as connected, they are more likely to pay attention to the quality of their relationships. So part of our work is to help develop an interdependent worldview in our employees. Leadership is about expanding the boundaries of thought, caring, and time horizons in our employees (Meadows, 2008).

We need to let go of the assumption that all of our assets are tangible. In the industrial economy, labor, capital, and natural resources were the organization's assets. Today, the notion of capital has expanded beyond money to intellectual capital, labor has morphed into talent and innovation, and human energy has been added to the intangible organizational assets that fuel a knowledge economy. Therefore, we need to replace our reliance on those traditional tangible assets with a new appreciation of our relationships with ideas, people, purpose, and the outside environment.

The quality and authenticity of the relationships between people, and between people and ideas, increase the flow of positive energy in organizations. Conversely, positive energy decreases when available energy is used for containment (silos) or self-protection (and self-interest). Connection that results in separation and self-protection reinforce boundaries. These kinds of boundaries decrease the energy flow between people (Allen & Mease, 2002).

Any transformation or organizational change requires energy. This energy can either be consumptive or generous. Consumptive change requires ongoing resources and energy to sustain the change. Generous change uses nature design principles that allow the intervention to disappear into the system. They don't require ongoing resources to maintain the change. This allows people (and their energy) to move to the next problem rather than having to maintain the previous solution.

The summary below shows how our focus would shift, what assumptions we would let go of, if we used nature's principle to "run on sunlight," and applied it to our organizations.

What do we need to focus on as leaders? What do we need to let go of?

1. **We need to encourage interconnections and interdependencies.**
   - *We need to let go of closed systems assumptions.*
   - *We need to let go of organizational mindsets built on seeing the organization as a machine.*

2. **We need to illuminate a shared higher purpose.**
   - *We need to let go of focusing on the parts instead of the whole.*

3. **We need to create conditions conducive to authentic relationships in the workplace.**

4. **We need to recognize the level of positive human energy as a key diagnostic of organizational health.**
   - *We need to let go of the assumption that all of our assets are tangible.*

Questions to Consider:

The idea that human beings can be a source of energy like sunlight is a provocative one. I recently read that researchers are developing a kind of fabric that will allow us to charge our electronics—just by wearing it. That would mean we are literally an energy source. However, in our organizations, human energy is still an unacknowledged asset. To foster and harvest human energy, we need to have an organizational photosynthesis process. We need a new way to think about leadership—as creating the conditions that allow positive human energy to be unleashed in service of the larger mission and purpose of the organization.

Here are some questions and areas of exploration to use as discussion points with our teams to further explore the concepts in this chapter.

- *What is the current level of positive energy that is being expressed in our organization?*
- *Are there pockets of positive energy within the organization, and if so, what can we learn from them?*
- *How might we integrate shared purpose, authentic relationships and reciprocity—critical photosynthetic elements to unleash positive human energy—into our performance reviews, hiring processes, our job descriptions and supervision?*
- *What conditions would support the formation of authentic relationships and what would they look like in our organizations?*
- *How might negative energy shift to positive energy in our organization?*
- *If we are already a wonderful place to work, how can we strengthen our intentionality to sustain this positive energy into the future?*
- *Is our current leadership literature and thinking influenced by a "non-living" system point of view? If so, do we need a new set leadership practices to tap this huge resource?*
- *How do we develop people in our organizations, who may have been brought up with a traditional view of leadership, so they can see a new way of being in an organization and have a different relationship with their supervisors and each other?*
- *How can we help our employees see the living system that they are a part of?*

CHAPTER THREE

In Nature Waste Is Never Wasted

When a giant redwood dies in the forest it continues to contribute to the forest ecology for five times the length of its lifetime. Its decomposing trunk, limbs and roots becomes food for other species in the forest, supporting the plants and trees that grow around it. The stump of the fallen tree becomes a nursing log for a new seedling to grow. The seed is not able to germinate in the shade under the ferns and other plant life close to the ground. But by germinating in the decomposing matter of the stump, it is raised above the forest floor allowing it to receive sunlight and flourish. Eventually the roots of the new tree grow around the stump to reach the ground.

These examples illustrate nature's highly efficient system of how it uses and reuses its resources. Nature is designed as an interdependent system and its ability to be waste free is predicated on connections between species in their ecosystem. The ability to use all available resources starts with how species in an ecological system relate to each other and how the waste of one can meet the needs of another. The lowly little dandelion is a champion at this. While dandelions are the bane of gardeners, only four percent of its scattered seeds actually take root. We might see the other 96% as wasted, but nature uses that "waste" to create build up in the soil so it can eventually nourish other plants.

When consumptive organizations resources are wasted, they are lost to the organization. The organization does not have the mindset or processes in place to recapture or recycle the waste to help it thrive. Consumptive organizations extract resources from their funders and employees and rarely count the cost or consider how to wisely use the resources to keep the company growing and thriving. For instance, they might ask an investor for start-up funds and use it all on developing a product without thinking of how some of it could be used to help sustain the business over time. Or they might have their employees work long hours without compensating them monetarily or with benefits, such as comp time, product discounts or stock options. Without some kind of recognition or reward, employees feel used, burned out and often end up leaving the organization taking important skills and institutional memory with them.

> *What if an organization's version of waste is never wasted?*

Some organizations have begun to apply nature's design principle in manufacturing redesigns that minimize or optimize waste. Usually when we attempt to eliminate waste in manufacturing, we focus on recycling and upcycling (McDonnough & Braungart; 2002 & 2013). Zero waste is a goal for organizations that are serious about the sustainable design of their products. But even as organizations try to redesign their products to be less wasteful, paradoxically, they rarely consider the waste in the human domain of the organization. We tend to have a high degree of tolerance for the waste that is a product of human behavior and the processes we create. To accurately get a sense of the cost of this, we need to be honest about the amount of wasted time and effort in our organizations. We also need to look deeply into how our human dynamics and leadership practices create waste in the form of dysfunction and drama.

When applied to an organization's culture, the "no waste is wasted" design principle changes the role of leadership. It causes leaders to focus on dynamics that usually only get dealt with when we reach a crisis point in an organization. Even then we often respond to the symptom and not the root cause. We need to be honest about the amount of wasted time and effort we have in our organizations. We also need to look deeply into how our human dynamics and leadership practices create waste in the form of dysfunction and drama.

The first step is to acknowledge what we waste. This helps us to name the problem and look for ways to create less waste. The following are some of the common ways we create waste in our organizations.

We waste time: Anyone who has sat through a meeting that didn't go anywhere can attest to an organization's ability to waste time. Meetings, while necessary, are often not optimized. We waste time when we habitually schedule meetings without identifying the purpose or even making sure they're necessary. We also waste time when we don't establish processes to address issues in a timely way and when we don't set a reasonable time limit for the meetings. When people are late to meetings; it is a waste of their colleague's time and costs the organization time and money as people wait for them before beginning the meeting. We also waste time and focus wondering about what is being decided behind closed doors, this is a cost associated with a lack of transparency.

We waste energy: Many of our processes are more complex than they need to be. Processes that are cumbersome or mysterious waste the energy of the staff. For instance, we all know the frustration of trying to navigate bureaucratic hoops and how it is not only a waste of time, but how the aggravation depletes us and seeps into our work dampening our creative energy.

How we relate to one another at work can also waste energy. When people don't cooperate with others or indulge in petty conflicts, it saps human energy. Negative attitudes among co-workers create an atmosphere of discontent and dissatisfaction which takes away from the positive human energy that organizations need to be at their best. When there is confusion about lines of responsibility or accountability, actions are often duplicated or run counter to the efforts of others, wasting energy on things that don't contribute to the larger mission of the organization.

We waste knowledge: The people in our organizations hold a wealth of perspectives and knowledge that can be valuable to our success and future. However, critical perspectives are often left out of the decision-making process because these staff people are not represented on the decision-making team. The knowledge of front-line staff, the people at the boundaries between the organization and its customers, is wasted if there isn't a way for them to share what they know. The decisions that are made without their input often lead to a "What were they thinking?" response from the front-line staff. This dynamic reinforces the sense that information and knowledge that resides throughout the organization isn't valued.

We also waste knowledge when it is privatized and not accessible to the organization. Some individuals seek job security by being the sole holder of key information. But when an individual's knowledge doesn't get passed on to others, it weakens the collective expertise. If the knowledge holder leaves the organization, their knowledge goes with them. The organization then wastes energy trying to reconstruct that knowledge. And if the system can't retrieve key information, it won't adapt as well to changes in the external environment. This increases the risk of a slow or maladaptive response and wastes opportunities that an integrated system could have captured.

We waste talents, skills and gifts: Many employees have talents, skills and gifts that are unknown to the organization and its managers and leaders. These "nutrients" can benefit the organization if the employee is willing to share them. But sometimes employees withhold skills in working environments where they don't feel appreciated, or have been burnt by how they have been treated, or sense a lack of integrity in the organization. For example, if an employee perceives that positional leaders are acting from self-interest rather than the interests of the whole organization, they become cautious or cynical. They show up to work and meet the minimum standards of the position, but they don't fully engage and share their ideas, skills, and expertise.

This self-protective act is wasteful to the living system because it can't access these resources. Decisions are made that could have been stronger if their skills and gifts were brought to the table. The person doing the withholding is also hurt as they do not feel fully engaged in the work (a sign of job satisfaction), and miss out on possible expanded roles and responsibilities and other advancements within the organization.

We waste capital, resources, and materials: Misguided human dynamics also exacerbate the waste of capital, resources and materials in our organizations. For example, if sales, service, and inventory employees have an ongoing conflict, it can result in gaps in the inventory needed to provide good service and can affect the reputation of the organization and its sales people. It can also generate waste through the extra time and energy needed to reschedule service delivery or having to create a larger inventory of parts to compensate for the human conflicts and still deliver on the organization's promises. This unnecessarily ties up organizational capital and can create opportunity costs due to lack of available capital and staff energy.

How does nature's lesson "that waste is never wasted" inspire us to think differently about leadership?

Traditionally, if we wanted to increase the productivity of our organizations, we focused on the number of items a person produces. In the early twentieth century, Frederick Taylor (1915) introduced time-motion studies that focused management on efficiency. He broke things down into parts along an assembly line and looked at ways to eliminate extraneous motion in an assembly-line worker's tasks. Later, time management studies taught us to eliminate time-wasting habits by focusing on top priorities, using a daily planner, and making use of every minute in the day (Covey, 1990). Each of these management trends focused on the relationship between the individual and the specific tasks they were trying to accomplish.

However, if we think about reducing waste or becoming waste free in a different context, it could lead us down a totally different path with amazing results in the productivity of the organization. Much of the waste in time, talent and knowledge in an organization come from the way the people manage themselves and the quality of the relationships between them. Optimizing the reduction of this kind of waste could be a very different way of unleashing the assets in our organizations.

A generous organization focuses on the system of interdependencies and relationships in their organization, designing ways for these interactions to work in a mutually-beneficial way for the people working there. By focusing on the following efforts and letting go of assumptions that do not serve us well, we can decrease the waste and unleash the talent throughout our organizations.

1. We need to develop the emotional intelligence of leaders and employees.

It is rare to find a graduate school that tells leaders that one of their key responsibilities is to develop their employees. However, this leadership practice is critical to reducing the waste found in the human dynamics of organizations. One important developmental area of focus is the emotional intelligence of the leaders and their employees (Goleman, 1995 &1997; Goleman et.al. 2002).

Organizations used to be places where rational thought predominated, and emotions were not allowed to be seen or heard. However, when we ask our employees to be passionate about their work, we open the door to their passion, as well as the emotions of frustration, excitement, anger, distrust, and boredom. Emotions travel faster than rational logic in networks (Goleman, 1995; Pert, 1999). These emotions aren't always expressed directly and can become part of a sub-culture or shadow culture in an organization. Think of a shadow culture, as all the conscious and unconscious non-official activities that help drive an organization: gossip around the water cooler, the after-meeting conversation in the parking lot, the playing of favorites. Accelerated by technology, such emotion-driven forces can multiply and powerful feelings—good or bad—can move exponentially faster and farther.

When a leader or an employee is not aware of their emotions and how they shape their behavior, they often behave in ways that drains the energy of others and wastes organizational time. In a generous organization, leaders create an organizational culture that supports the development of emotional intelligence. Paying attention to emotional intelligence in employees and the collective organization is one shift that leaders in living systems need to make.

We need to let go of unmanaged responses to our emotions. Controlling behaviors can be counterproductive, often we find that fear and distrust drive these actions. Sometimes people who are overly controlling or who advocate a seemingly inappropriate position in a meeting aren't even aware that their emotions are influencing their decisions. These emotions need to be named and managed and we need to make it clear that we do not tolerate the negative behaviors associated with them.

For example, I once worked with a leadership team where every member had been touched by alcoholism in their family system. The ones who were emotionally intelligent had learned to address the issues this raised for them and didn't bring this experience into the organization. However, the ones who were not as self-aware tended to create highly controlling processes in their areas of responsibility. For them, chaos was dangerous, so they sought safety in control. Even though they had a rational explanation for why they created each policy and process, these individuals' behaviors were being driven by their unconscious emotions and drained the energy and time of their colleagues and the organization. The rest of the staff did not share their fear. To these other staff members, the control represented a lack of flexibility and hindered their ability to do their jobs at the highest level. To make matters worse, the high level leadership positions of these controlling individuals amplified the consequences of their behavior. The answer to this challenge was to help them build their emotional intelligence and to see how the history of their family systems were showing up at work.

To some the idea of addressing emotional intelligence may seem like quite a challenge and outside of the purview of our organizations, but it is possible to do this in a non-threatening and effective way. For example, one of my clients has supported a youth group in St. Paul to increase their emotional intelligence. This group has been so successful at calling each other out on their *emotional highjacks* that they have been asked to speak at schools and organizations to help others learn how to do the same. Recently one of the members of this youth group talked about his growing skills to recognize his anger and manage his emotional reaction to what he was experiencing in his life. His issues and challenges haven't disappeared, but his reactions to them have shifted dramatically. He can now recognize what his feelings are, acknowledge them, and choose from a range of behaviors to respond.

We need to let go of dysfunctional behavior and the denial of its costs. Organizations, departments, teams, individuals and leaders themselves can be dysfunctional. I often hear stories about leaders who get angry and direct their anger to whoever happens to be nearby. Everyone puts their heads down and acts as if the behavior is acceptable. This habit consumes time, energy and focus and makes everything about the CEO, not the organization's mission. We need to let go of our tolerance for this kind of behavior and learn to name the emotions that are present.

Our lack of action, in part, relates to our denial of the costs. We seem to think, "If I don't name the dysfunction and drama, it doesn't exist, and I don't have to act to change it." But this is obviously not true, and the costs of this kind of denial to each other, the organization, our bottom line, our customers and the environment are great. The stories of these dysfunctions often take up time and energy as they occupy water cooler talks, venting sessions with friends, and complaints with colleagues. As leaders, we need to let go of our tolerance for dysfunction.

2. We need to cultivate a culture of transparency.

People are curious, and when there is a perception (or reality) of secrecy in an organization, it draws attention. They say that nature abhors a vacuum and proceeds to fill it. In organizations, in the absence of openness and information, people run in to fill it! Employees will make something up that fits their perceptions and contribute it to the rumor mill. These rumor mills occupy employees' time and attention and take them away from delivering on the organizational mission. Anyone who follows social media and fake items on the Internet understands how false information can be spread by human beings through their networks. This dynamic is very like the impact of rumors in our organizations. Rumors or false assertions are damaging to our organization's culture and relationships and take our time and attention away from other areas of focus.

> *Cultivating a culture of trust and transparency is a powerful way to eliminate the waste of energy and time.*

We need to let go of our unexamined defaults and secrecy. Whenever there is a diminishment of trust and flow of information, people must work harder to produce the same or lower results. Transparency grows trust. Sharing information freely helps the organization to adapt. And the lack of transparency has its costs. This cost gets magnified when there is a lack of trust in the leadership of an organization. The lack of trust, combined with a lack of transparency, creates an exponential energy drain for an organization (Lyman, 2012). People withdraw their positive energy and withhold their active cooperation, sometimes without even being conscious of it. The waste of time and energy can't be measured.

There are often unexamined defaults of what needs to be kept secret in the organization. We may think because something used to be confidential that it still is. Leaders need to reexamine their rules regarding secrecy to see if they still serve the organization, or if they create unintended negative consequences. Other kinds of secrecy get linked to confidential issues that are driven by laws or outside regulators. Taking the time to name the rules of secrecy that the organization holds would be a start for shifting an organization's culture toward transparency.

An example of the cost due to a lack of trust and transparency occurred at a college I worked with. A new president was hired using a closed process in a college that had a culture of candor and openness. Not long into the president's tenure, a rumor started that the faculty's discount at the college bookstore was going to be eliminated. This rumor took hold and spread throughout the faculty. The number of calls, visits, and emails checking to see if this was true created a huge waste, particularly since it wasn't true.

This scenario demonstrates a principle from chaos theory called "sensitive dependence on initial conditions" (Gleick, 1987). In an interdependent system, the flap of a butterfly's wings in China can create a snow storm in New York. It also explains the angst created in the faculty and how it grew. Low transparency and trust created an initial condition where any rumor was treated as fact. We need to let go of the defaults that support closed-door secrecy.

3. We need to set a low level of tolerance for organizational waste.

There is huge waste in the human dynamics of our organizations. The reason it persists is that we have a high tolerance and an almost fatalistic attitude that this waste of time, knowledge, energy and talent is normal and can't be changed. Part of developing a lower tolerance for waste is a shift in our mindset. One of the changes that helped drive the recycling movement was letting go of a throwaway mentality. We didn't pay attention to it until we made the connection between what we throwaway and the cost to the environment in landfills. Once the consequences of our throwaway habits became known and understood, we began to change our behavior and started recycling. It took a while to build up the infrastructure to support this shift, but now many individuals have recycling bins at home and are diminishing their contributions to landfills.

> *In our organizations, we continually throw away people, knowledge, talent, wisdom, and time. We need to shift to a mentality where the short and long-term costs of our actions are considered before we act.*

Our organizations need to decrease their tolerance for wasting employee's time and energy. As described above, meetings are a big culprit of this. But the tolerance we have for this waste is legendary, part of this is because we don't have metrics for measuring the energy waste in our meetings. One example of such a metric would be to count the total salaried/hourly costs of the people attending the meeting. If we had the total worth of the time of the employees in the meeting, we could ask at the end of the meeting: "Did this investment of time serve the company?" This simple tweak in our standard operating procedures could raise awareness of how we use meetings and how much dysfunctional meetings cost the organization. If we ask these questions each time we attended a meeting, the individual and collective consciousness of our behavior would make us more disciplined at reducing waste in meetings. And our tolerance of late comers, or inattentive participants, or the person who wants to talk all the time, would diminish.

I once worked with a president of a large community college who wanted to create a healthier organization and decided to experiment with an intervention.

He invested in facilitation training for everyone who ran meetings at the college. This facilitation capacity enhanced the quality of every meeting that was held on the campus. It increased the equity of participation, the focus on topic, and the decision-making at meetings. It was a simple intervention with great rewards. Initially, it decreased the tolerance for the status quo and then eventually led to new demands for meaning and rigor in meetings.

4. We need to design systems that strengthen the development of human capacity.

One way that nature eliminates waste is through the cycling of resources and nutrients in an ecological system. As mentioned above, our organizations are filled with talent, gifts, and potential that are sometime seen and appreciated but more often they are hidden, withheld, or unnoticed by others. If we can actively grow and develop people, we will build adaptive capacity in our organizations and a greater capacity to carry on important work over time (Allen, et. al. 1998).

The talent management trend is an example of resource cycling in human organizations (Smart, 2005; Keller & Price, 2011). The emergence of this trend isn't a coincidence; it's a recognition that our talent is a critical asset in a knowledge economy. Some organizations intentionally focus on growing their own employees to fill key talent goals. For example, a rural community in Nebraska encourages their high school graduates to return by integrating them back into the town after college as employees and business owners to support the sustainability of their community. Many of their high school graduates come back to this town because they grew up with a lifestyle that they appreciate, and they want their children to experience. The local community foundation has a tag line that reflects this strategy. They say, "we recycle people" in our community. Some colleges have used a similar strategy to create greater diversity in their faculty and administrative staff by encouraging students who have gone to school there to come back and teach or work after they finish their graduate work.

5. We need to design systems that intentionally pass on individual wisdom and knowledge to others in the organization.

In indigenous populations, the elders hold the knowledge and history of their community, such as how they survived in a 100-year flood or disaster. The community looks to them for help when natural disasters hit their village. This is also the tradition behind the living bridges of Meghalaya, where the elders share the wisdom and skills of creating the bridges with the next generations so as to sustain this practice and ensure the well-being of their communities.

But our transitions and processes typically aren't focused on intentionally passing on individual wisdom so that it is accessible to the next generation of people who will work in the organization. Our consumptive organizations see transitions as "out with the old and in with the new." This often creates a hard edge to the transition and much is lost for the individual and the organization. Even a short overlap of the retiring or exiting leader with the incoming leader doesn't allow for the deeper wisdom and knowledge to be shared over time and as the need for that knowledge arises (Dixon, 2000).

Nature's design is to build redundancy for all critical functions, so if one fails there is always a backup. The redundancy isn't necessarily efficient in the short-run, but it is effective and builds resilience for the ecosystem. In our organizations, the redundancy of passing on knowledge is best done before the departure of key people. One way to ensure this redundancy is to develop "bench strength" for people in critical positions. This means identifying people who can take on responsibilities if a colleague who holds a critical position gets injured or leaves the organization.

Sharing information and coaching individuals on a day-to-day basis also builds knowledge strength in the organization over time. There are ways that organizations can encourage this behavior. For example, a colleague of mine who was a vice president of a large financial firm had 25% of his bonus tied to his ability to coach his direct reports. His direct reports were asked at the end of the year about the quantity and quality of coaching they received from their boss and their responses determined the amount of his bonus.

We need to let go of the practice of privatizing knowledge and assets. In the mechanistic paradigm of organizations, we focused on the individual parts of the organization. Components could be broken down and reassembled and parts could be replaced or repaired. The sum of the parts equaled the sum of the whole. This framework was also applied to the individuals in the organization. An employee could privatize their own knowledge or that of their department to serve their self-interest.

In a living system, the whole is more than the sum of its parts. There are always emergent properties (things that exist only in the whole and aren't found in the individual parts) that arise out of the interactions of the parts of the system. Therefore, there is a cost to privatizing knowledge in a living system, the information is needed for the system to adapt and learn. When this information is restricted it diminishes the feedback needed for the individuals and the organization to evolve.

An example of the benefits of shared information and knowledge comes from a colleague who created the Prince Henry Award in his organization. Prince Henry the Navigator was the third son of King John I of Portugal in the 1400s. At that time, Portugal was a shipping empire and, yet all the ship captains had their own proprietary maps of the world. Prince Henry collected all these maps and created a map that integrated all of this knowledge. He then gave this integrated map back to each ship captain with the following instructions: Explore, learn and then come back and teach what you have learned to others. My colleague used this story to reward the team that honored these principles by doing the best job of exploring the edges of their practice, learning from their experiments and innovations, and sharing what they learned with other teams in the organization. This process encourages a culture of sharing learning throughout the organization so it is held in the collective memory of the organization instead of an individual's mind.

The summary below shows how our focus would shift, what assumptions we would let go of, if we used nature's principle "waste is never wasted," and applied it to our organizations.

What do we need to focus on as leaders? What do we need to let go of?

1. We need to develop the emotional intelligence of leaders and employees.
   - *We need to let go of unmanaged responses to our emotions.*
   - *We need to let go of dysfunctional behavior and the denial of its costs.*

2. We need to cultivate a culture of transparency.
   - *We need to let go of our unexamined defaults and secrecy.*

3. We need to set a low level of tolerance for organizational waste.

4. We need to design systems that strengthen the development of human capacity.

5. We need to design systems that intentionally pass on individual wisdom and knowledge to others in the organization.
   - *We need to let go of the practice of privatizing knowledge and assets.*

Questions to Consider:

We can't minimize waste if we don't recognize and name it. To understand where the waste is in our organizations, we need to bring together a people who represent a cross section of the organization. And then have a facilitated conversation using the following questions to identify where there is excess waste in the organization and what we might do address it.

- *Where do we have examples of:*
- *wasted time?*
- *wasted knowledge?*
- *wasted wisdom?*
- *wasted money?*
- *wasted power?*
- *wasted energy?*
- *wasted talent?*
- *Now that we have named what we waste, what is the smallest thing we can do to diminish this waste?*
- *How can we foster the wise use of our resources and diminish waste in our system?*
- *What kind of action could trigger an awareness of the wasteful consequences of our actions in meetings?*

CHAPTER FOUR

Nature Fits Form to Function

The living bridges of Meghalaya are a beautiful example of form following function. The form of the bridge evolves as the roots of the tree grow into a living bridge. The living bridge becomes stronger and more complex as it ages, just like all living beings.

In nature, the form always serves the primary function the species or ecosystem. You can pick any plant, animal, insect or living thing and discover how its form helps it survive and thrive by finding the best fit with its environment. Nature has many examples of how form fits function. Kangaroos have joey pouches to protect their young while they bounce from place to place. Lotus flowers have tiny bumps that inhibit dirt and microorganism from sticking to its surface which helps it stay clean in a muddy environment.

Water is another example of form fitting function. While water doesn't have consciousness; it has much to teach us in how it seamlessly shifts its form to adapt to the terrain it faces. Gravity shapes the direction of water, drawing it toward sea level. Over the miles, the water's form changes as it encounters obstacles in its path. The Mississippi River starts in northern Minnesota where it is shallow; you can walk across its headwaters. As the water flows to the Gulf of Mexico, it takes on many forms from waterfalls to rapids, to winding curves and finally to a wide lazy river. This fluid shifting of form to support the function, also applies to human beings. For example, our form of communication as a two-year old evolves and becomes more sophisticated as we grow.

But there are also instances when things aren't allowed to evolve in this way, for instance, in consumptive organizations the lesson of fitting form to function isn't practiced. They do not recognize that while the initial form may have once served the organization's purpose, as the organization grows, and the market and other external factors change, the form needs to change as well. Their attachment to the initial form clouds their judgement and doesn't serve the organization's evolving purpose. Generous organizations, on the other hand, seamlessly adapt its forms to fit the evolving and larger purpose of the organization, as the external environment changes around the organization.

The Cycle of Form and Function:

When we see organizations as living systems, we can begin to identify the dynamics and cycles that these living systems exemplify. One of these dynamics is panarchy (Gunderson & Holling, 2002). Panarchy identifies the deep patterns that occur in the transformation cycles that living systems (natural and human) go through. In the initial "growth" phase, an organization develops a business plan, builds up the needed resources, and launches a successful enterprise. In the next "conservation" phase, the organization moves to launch their product and solidify their market niche. At this point, they are successfully producing their product (the form matches the function they need) and things become systemized. But when the system becomes so set that it ceases to adapt to changing conditions, the rigidity of the form triggers a collapse. If they are to be successful, the company must be adaptive and explore other options or designs which allow resources to be reorganized so that the system adapts or resets to the changing condition.

Nature also runs on panarchy. I visited Yellowstone National Park the spring after the big fires in 1988. I was amazed to see so much green growing from the charred remains of the trees in the park. I learned that certain pine trees have seeds that only crack open under intense heat. It is nature's way of resetting the system from a catastrophic collapse of a forest due to fire.

This cycle is a demonstration of the relationship between form and function. The function or purpose is set and the forms are created to facilitate the function. Another example comes from the gecko. As more land animals created a competitive environment on the ground, it needed to adapt in order to survive. The adaption took on the form of sticky feet that enables it to climb trees and plants vertically, to find an environmental niche where it can thrive (Allen, 2010).

In human organizations and communities there is a constant evolution occurring. In business, disruptive technologies are occurring all the time, even if we can't see them coming (Bower & Christensen, 1995; Kiuchi & Shireman, 2002). Disruptive technologies are innovations that create new markets and eventually disrupt an existing market which in turn, displaces an established product or market. These innovations often trigger the collapse of an organization's business model. A firm is ripe for disruption when they become too rigid in their approach to their market or product. Rigidity in thinking or form means that the company is not adapting to external forces and when they don't adapt, others will innovate and disrupt their product.

For example, photography used to be attached to film, but the innovation of digital photography completely disrupted the photographic film industry. Digital watches disrupted analogue watches and self-driving cars are bound to disrupt the insurance industry, the design of roads, urban planning, commuting habits and more. Just as Uber disrupted the taxi industry and Trip Advisor and Airbnb disrupted the hospitality industry. Examples of innovations driven by technology are accelerating, more and more. To remain relevant a company needs to constantly adapt its forms to deliver on their purpose.

How does nature's lesson of "fitting form to function" help us to think differently about leadership?

There are many examples of small tweaks, large changes, or acts of letting go that help programs adapt to what they are learning and be more responsive to changes in the environment. Sometimes these have led to a reorganization of a company or caused its demise. Despite this reality, and numerous books on building cultures of innovation and adaptation, we have yet to successfully create seamless shifts in organizational forms (processes and procedures) to serve the higher purpose the organization it is there to serve.

1. We need to think in ecocycles:

Organizations are built on structures, but living systems aren't just structures they are also movements. These movements have a pattern of adaptive cycles such as panarchy or ecocycles. An ecocycle is a framework for understanding movements and cycles in living systems and for applying it to planning and leading (Hurst, 2012; Kiuchi & Shireman, 2002; Lipmanowicz & McCandless, 2013). The ecocycle below is adapted from *The Surprising Power of Liberating Structures: Simple rules to unleash a culture of innovation* (Lipmanowicz & McCandless 2014).

The ecocycle shows four main phases cycling through an infinity loop. The front loop is the development to maturity arc. We launch new products or processes and grow them to maturity. The maturity phase is where we stabilize, standardize, and maintain our products. The back loop starts with a crisis or collapse of a business model. This triggers a release of resources and takes us into the exploration phase, where the released resources are used to explore innovative ideas that make the organization more adaptive. This adaptive cycle is what makes living systems resilient.

Consumptive organizations see planning as a linear event. Goals and objectives are set and accomplished over a 1-3-year timeframe. Often goals are made up of three categories: things to initiate, problems to be solved, and things to be maintained. Unlike the ecocycle, there is no release stage in a linear framework. The things that are initiated in the first year become problems to solve in the second year and maintenance goals in the third. Within the first three

ECOCYCLE PLANNING

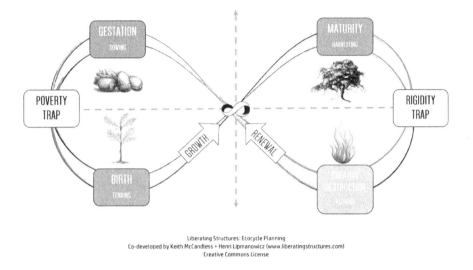

Liberating Structures: Ecocycle Planning
Co-developed by Keith McCandless + Henri Lipmanowicz (www.liberatingstructures.com)
Creative Commons License

years, the majority of the time is spent maintaining goals that consume energy and discourage people from adapting to changes in the external environment. They already have enough to do holding things in place and don't have the resources or energy to continue to innovate.

Generous organizations create a space for an adaptive cycle, like the ecocycle above, which invites an intentional letting go of all preconceived assumptions or structures to release new energy and resources. These resources are then used to explore and launch new products or thinking. The ecocycle allows for a deeper adaptation and a letting go to drive the next innovation. To generate a new ecocycle, we need to ask ourselves:

- *What needs to be explored?*
- *What needs to be launched?*
- *What needs to be sustained and systematized?*
- *What needs to be let go of or released to make room for the next innovation?*

2. We need to cultivate a culture of adaptation.

Can you imagine how long an animal would survive if it stood outside its den studying and planning how to identify the perfect food source? I once worked with an organization that wanted everything to be perfect. It had the luxury to spend a lot of time in planning before they launched anything. The problem was that the world was passing them by. In addition, by the time the product was launched, the amount of time and funds sunk into it made it difficult for people to let go of it even if it didn't live up to its purpose or promise. As part of an organizational change effort, we replaced the goal of perfection with experimentation. By allowing things to be framed as an experiment, the lead time between idea and launch shortened dramatically. Learning from the experiment and making changes based on that learning created rapid cycles of adaption, like water flowing downstream towards sea level.

This is one way to create a culture of adaptation in an organization. The use of experimentation allows for pilot forms to exist that are easily changed to serve the purpose. Nature has been running an experiment on this planet for billions of years, and life forms are still constantly changing and experimenting! Being adaptive, experimental and looking toward the long haul is something we could learn from nature.

Another strategy is to introduce migration as a metaphor for evolving forms. In nature, species that migrate from winter to summer habitats and back again stay alive and thrive. They move to where the resources (food, water, etc.) are abundant. The migration allows for a life cycle of adaptation embedded in a journey from one place to another.

I have found the migration metaphor helpful when moving an organization from traditional to emergent practice. It invites staff members to envision their work as heading toward a destination point. The destination (purpose) is clear but getting there may involve detours and learning along the way. When we migrate from one way of doing things to another, it can open additional ways to move forward. It doesn't need to happen all at once, the journey allows people to have the time to adjust their habits, thinking, and practice.

In other instances, species change forms as they mature. The walking stick is an example of an insect that changes forms as it grows. Initially it goes from egg to nymph. The nymph is green and will shed its skin several times before becoming an adult. When it becomes an adult, the walking stick is twig brown which allows it to blend into the branches of trees during the day and feed at night.

Unlike the walking stick, many organizations are resistant to changing forms, they hold fast to their traditional ways of doing business. For example, I worked with a family-owned business that was growing rapidly. They needed to think strategically and generate financial data that would help them see true costs, aid in decision-making, and understand the cost of not investing in the future of the business. One of the habits that made them successful as a small family business is that when a request for proposal for new business came in, they dropped everything and worked on the bid. While this worked when they were small, it took their attention away from strategy, personnel issues, and the technology investments that they needed to sustain their growth. The leaders of this business needed to develop more consciousness about their default behaviors and understand how they did not serve their future stability and growth. They had to go beyond the present time frame and their reluctance to invest in needed equipment and infrastructure. They needed to let go of scarcity as a mentality and shift to an investment to grow strategy (much like shrubs and perennials choose to invest in their root structure).

George Land in his book *Grow or Die: The unifying principle of transformation* identifies the growth cycles that organizations move through (1986). The first is entrepreneurship where they experiment, invent and launch their business. Next, they standardize business processes and production. Then they enter a third phase of diversification and integration. What is powerful about Land's concept of transformation is that the structure, assumptions, habits and thinking of each phase must be replaced with new thinking to succeed in the next phase. This is a good example of form fits function. As an organization evolves, things that worked earlier in its evolution do not necessarily fit as it grows. When businesses don't let go of their default behavior, they can't maintain the growth and will fall back to earlier levels of earning. This principle is basic and universal and is seen in all biological, chemical, physical, psychological and cultural processes (Land, 1986).

We need to let go of "That's how we've always done it" thinking. We have all been in meetings where the phrase "we've always done it this way" has been said. In the twentieth century, this phrase used to stop alternative thinking in its tracks. Today, it is easier to push back. Previously, I gave several examples of disruptive technologies that have turned businesses upside down. Any business that is driven by technology understands that they need to let go at the peak of success to innovate. The risks of not letting go of what we know are that someone else in the field is inventing the disruptions that will (Kelly, 1998). As leaders, we need to focus on these default practices and the thinking behind them and lift them up so they can be examined to see if our beliefs remain relevant or if we need to let go of them.

3. We need clarity of purpose and function.

In nature, the higher purpose is to live; all species are focused on thriving right now and for generations to come. In an organization, our function is also found in our purpose, but the purpose is not always as well-defined (Meadows, 2008). When people don't have a clear purpose, they rely on forms to "hold them to task" such as eight-hour workdays and mandatory requirements for coming into the office, etc. But when a person is clear about their function and purpose, the form of the organization matters less. Remote working, desk sharing, flexible hours are all forms that work best when the employees have clarity of purpose and function. The same is true for organizations that rely on distributed leadership.

> *How do you determine the purpose of the leadership team*
> *or an organizational process?*

Purpose is interesting, because many times it gets lost in the focus on the *how, who or what* instead of the *why*. Clarity of purpose arises from the articulation of the deep need the organization is trying to meet (Hock, 1999). When I work with leadership groups who want to become a high-performance team the first task I give them is to name the deep need they are there to fulfill for the organization. Sometimes it is surprisingly difficult for the individuals to name this deep need. But if they are unable to articulate this it indicates that their leadership team's purpose statements aren't anchored in deep meaning. A purpose without roots is easily ignored and doesn't shape the behavior of the team or process.

Peter Vaill's *Purposing of High-performing Systems* uses purposing rather than purpose to communicate the ongoing need to identify what the team is there to serve. He defines purposing as "(the) continuous stream of actions by an organization's formal leadership which have the effect of inducing clarity, consensus, and commitment regarding the organization's basic purposes" (Vaill, 1980, p. 91). In his research, this behavior of continuing to clarify purposing is linked to the team's ability to be high-performing.

The Benedictine Order of the Catholic Church uses different language and practice to focus on purpose. They have a 1,500-year tradition of living in communities that sustain their purpose. Benedictines have figured out how to optimize tensions in order to sustain a vital community over time. One of these tensions is conversation and stability. They see their core values as providing stability over 1,500 years and they invite ongoing conversations with the newest members of their community to see how these values will be lived out as society and needs change. Their stability embedded in core values is their version of function and purpose, while conversation is the process that allows the forms to adapt as their community evolves and the members change.

Our leadership challenge is to focus our organizations on purpose and function. As this purpose is strengthened and highlighted, it will make it easier to see when the forms for achieving this purpose no longer fit the function. Thereby, allowing the organization to respond to the feedback that tells them it is time to seamlessly shift to a more adaptive form.

4. We need to focus on emergent practice.

Organizations often embed form into its structures and processes. This makes the forms more rigid, resistant to change, and requires more work to adapt to a new form that supports the function of the organization. For example, we love the idea of best practice. Once a best practice has been identified in an organization, protocols are established to ensure that everyone in the organization is following them. I often find this is the case with government contracts. While this may work for the funding organizations, the people receiving these contracts are in the field continually experimenting with the best way to serve their clients or business, as opposed to strictly following some best practice designed by someone outside of their local area and expertise. They are adapting to what is changing in the lives of their clients and the environment. Instead of supporting this innovation, state and federal contracts tend to lock their funding into best practices whether they are the best fit or not.

Ironically, as illustrated above, pursuing best practice is an indicator that you are approaching a rigid form. Best practice, by definition, looks at what has worked in the past. It articulates and encodes the best practice as if, once identified, this practice will hold for the rest of time and for every situation and location. This goes against our intuitive understanding that the context in which we practice is always changing. The aspiration behind best practice is to do excellent work. However, to do excellent work we must let go of best practices and seek ongoing adaptation and innovation.

The nature of the non-linear dynamics of an open living system fits with emergent practice rather than best or good practice. Living systems are open systems which means that variables keep expanding and other things in the external environment continually show up. The only way to develop a response to all these different variables is to develop strategies from the patterns that emerge from complex situations. Living systems develop an emergent practice approach to decision-making (Snowden & Boone, 2007).

Emergent practice is all about adaptation and experimentation. Because the unknowns are unknown, this world view invites a more natural response to the relationship between form and function. Emergent practice allows for the ongoing search for the best "fit" to a problem so the "form" is always assessed based on its ability to serve the higher purpose of the organization.

> *Leaders who are interested in creating a culture of adaptation and innovation need to help their organization understand and embrace emergent practice.*

We need to let go of our attachments to specific forms. As leaders, we seek adaptation and innovation through the focus on function and the letting go of forms that no longer fit. We also need to notice organizational and individual habits that protect forms. Sometimes individuals get attached to a specific form because it satisfies an emotional need that they may or may not be aware of. Individual egos can also attach to a specific form that hinders the adaptive capacity of an organization. Perhaps an individual was instrumental in creating a process or protocol. Maybe they are proud of what they created and believe their form is the one right way to do the work. This causes the ego to engage when others suggest changes in the way something should be done in the organization. The ego of the individual defends the "form" and if that individual is in a position of organizational power, it hinders the organization's ability to adapt. As leaders, we need to focus on the emotions and egos of our employees and ourselves to see if they are inadvertently hurting the organization's ability to deliver on its purpose.

Nature creates rich and diverse feedback loops that reinforce or balance the system. If employees are focused only on their job, they aren't noticing the feedback that is coming from other parts of the organization or the external environments that are giving information about our practices and forms. We also need to let go of the habit of only seeing the part, not the whole. This habit protects the form, not the function.

5. We need to recognize when form no longer follows function and adapt accordingly.

A living organization will give us feedback when a form no longer fits its function. Ants alter their foraging behavior when the food source runs out. But our busy minds and emotions can cause us to resist or ignore feedback. As leaders, we need to focus on feedback and what it is telling us about how well our forms fit their functions. When form no longer follows function three things happen.

1. It takes longer to complete a task or goal than it used to,
2. It takes more time or people to accomplish the same thing, or
3. It takes more resources to accomplish the same or less (Lynch & Kordis, 1988).

Leading a living system requires the people in it to notice when these three symptoms are present; to pay attention to the waste of energy or when too much energy is needed to do something. In Lynch and Kordis's book *Strategy of the Dolphin: Scoring a Win in a Chaotic World* (1988) they use the dolphin as a model and mentor for shifting forms. The dolphin jumps from wave to wave, using the energy of the building wave to jump to the next wave. They don't follow the wave on the downward trajectory. They let go to keep their momentum going.

Another way to anticipate the need to shift forms in a living organization is to embed environmental scanning capacity at all levels of the organization and facilitate the collecting and processing of this information into patterns. This pattern recognition will give a living human organization a way to notice feedback that the external environment is providing and anticipate the need to shift forms (Allen & Cherrey, 2000).

We need to let go of filters that limit information. There is a lot of information that comes at us on any day. For example, a weekday edition of The New York Times contains more information than the average person was likely to come across in a lifetime in seventeenth-century England (Wurman, 1989). The amount of data and information (feedback) that exists in the world is voluminous and it's increasing each and every day. The challenge isn't to eliminate information, but to create filters that categorize information and process it into knowledge that we need to pay attention to (Brockman, 2015: Rosen, 2015). The challenge is creating filters that don't bias us against the feedback that we need. To deliver our highest purpose, we need to be both intentional and open (to surprise) about the information we seek.

Nature operates at different time scales in adapting how form changes to fit function. Sometimes it acts from moment to moment like a chameleon changing colors. Form can also be adjusted seasonally like dogs that shed their winter coat when it warms up and the artic fox whose fur changes from white and blue in the winter to red-brown in the summer to better sneak up on prey and hide from predators. Nature also takes the long view of evolution. A species that no longer fits due to their habitat changing faster than they can adapt their form will die off because they could not perform their core function of survival.

If we want to grow generous organizations, we need to create environments that strengthen the clarity and commitment to the core function (big or small) in the organization. This allows for weak forms to exist in the organization, forms that will shift quickly and smoothly so the core function continues to be met. Living organizations that have strong purposes and fluid forms will be more adaptive.

> *Does the form fit the function, and does it consider*
> *the uniqueness of the context?*

This is the leadership question for generous organizations that want to thrive in today's world. We are on a journey to understand what this means in our organizations and what it means to lead an organization that always places purpose and function first. To prioritize function means that our forms need to seamlessly shift to meet the demands of our changing environment. Leaders need to help the organization and the people in it to adapt to new practices and let go of others to make this shift.

The summary below shows how our focus would shift, what assumptions we would let go of, if we used nature's principle "fit form to function" and applied it to our organizations.

What do we need to focus on as leaders? What do we need to let go of?

1. We need to think in ecocycles.

2. We need to cultivate a culture of adaptation.
   - *We need to let go of "That's how we've always done it" thinking.*

3. We need clarity of purpose and function.

4. We need to focus on emergent practice.
   - *We need to let go of our attachments to specific forms.*

5. We need to recognize when form no longer follows function and adapt accordingly.
   - *We need to let go of filters that limit information.*

Questions to Consider:

Nature is elegant and optimal in fitting form to function. A plant stem serves to scaffold, store, transport and generate via one simple device. Organizations often create forms that originally fit a function, but as the external environment or internal conditions evolve, the form becomes a hindrance to achieving the function instead of the original help it provided. If we want to experiment with this design principle from nature, I would suggest that we reflect on the following questions.

- *Why are we humans so prone to prioritizing form over function?*
- *Is "purpose" the optimal function of organizations and communities?*
- *The external environment is dynamic and turbulent, therefore our organizational forms "should" be constantly evolving to maintain function. How do we let go of forms that no longer work in our organization, or are taking up more energy than they need to?*
- *How can leaders create nimble forms, such as those found in living systems, and use them to adapt to changing functions?*
- *What is the purpose of the leadership team? Is it clear and does the form of the leadership team continues to evolve to maintain its fit to function?*
- *What is the purpose of an organizational process?*
- *Does the form fit the function and does it consider the uniqueness of the context?*

CHAPTER FIVE

Nature Rewards Cooperation

Mycelium is a mushroom whose "job description" is to model a system that exemplifies collaboration in nature (Stamets, 2005). Through their extensive roots, mycelium facilitates the flow of nutrients between species, shares information, and connects species in the forest. Using the interconnecting web of mycelium roots, a tree can direct specific nutrients to a seedling hundreds of feet away. Or a plant that is under attack from a pest can use the mycelium's roots to communicate that information to other plants that may be threatened. If we were to use nature as a mentor, we could look to mycelium as a model of innovative strategies for designing collaborations that are mutually beneficial for all involved. It is also an example of how Type III ecologies are highly evolved and designed to encourage these mutually-beneficial relationships.

There are also generous mutualistic relationships in business. Open Source software development is an example of the kind of cooperation found in Type

III ecologies in nature. Open Source is founded on the freedom to use the work, study the work, copy and share the work, and modify the work. It isn't a copyright; rather it is a "copyleft." Copyleft is a familiar term in the software world and indicates an arrangement whereby software or artistic work may be used, modified, and distributed freely on condition that anything derived from it is bound by the same condition.[3] In Open Source, people have many roles including core developers, maintainers, patchers, bug reporters, and documenters. People in these roles freely give their time and talents to the project. This gift economy continues to develop Open Source software to be used by businesses today. Currently 76% of businesses run on or use some form of Open Source software.

The Leadership Learning Community[4] is another example of a generous organization. The organization is run on the contributions of people who are willing to show up and share their knowledge. It brings together funders who support leadership development programs, the alumni of these programs, and the consultants that facilitate and teach in these programs. The goal is to use their knowledge and experiences to accelerate the knowledge and skills needed to develop leadership in this world. This gift economy is another example of how human organizations are operating in a similar way to the mutualistic and generous Type III ecologies.

In addition, we have all heard stories from colleagues who work in great organizations. They usually talk about the level of trust and cooperation they experience daily. They see how their contributions help others and the organization and, in turn, are helped by others as well. They don't drain energy, time, or organizational resources to get things done. In other words, they contribute back to the soil—to the nutrients that help to support everyone—instead of taking from it.

As a participant in annual budgeting for many years, I can see how the organizations I have worked in reflect the distinct types of ecological stages. Some organizations budget like Type I ecologies, where people and departments (like annuals and weeds) look to the organization to give them all the resources

[3] https://www.google.com/search?q=copyleft&ie=utf-8&oe=utf-8 4 http://leadershiplearning.org/
[4] http://leadershiplearning.org/

they need and feel no obligation to give back. These organizations usually have a short life. Other organizations are like Type II ecologies where departments (like perennials and shrubs) do not use all the resources but invest some of the organizational resources in themselves. They last longer but still take more than they give back. The generous organization, like those organizations described previously, is like Type III ecology; the people in it sustain each other and as a result give back to the organization instead of draining it of its resources. The generous organization, like those organizations described above, is like Type III ecology; the people in it sustain each other and as a result give back to the organization instead of draining it of its resources.

There are two reasons why consumptive organizations don't serve us as well. The first is that these days our organizations are living networks – just like nature—and as such are interdependent and connected. Technology has connected us across and outside our organizations making them more permeable (Allen & Cherrey, 2000). The dynamics of this structure builds interdependence, information and emotion flow in a way that didn't exist in the 1950s (Baker, 2014). The second reason is that over the last 20 years the knowledge economy has created the first infinite organizational resource—the internet (Halal, 1998). In this knowledge era, for the first time in our organizational history, collaboration has become economically efficient (Halal, 1998). It is through collaboration that new knowledge grows.

Coral reefs are a perfect example of the complex and symbiotic relationship that exists in generous Type III ecologies:

> Between one to nine million species are estimated to live on coral reefs. Some species spend their entire life on a reef. Others, like sharks, Jacks and manta rays are just visitors that come to the reef to feed, be groomed by cleaner fish or other reasons.... Coral polyps are simple animals that live within a protective calcium carbonate shell. They grow into rock-like colonies which form the basic structure of a coral reef. Polyps are only able to do this because they have formed a symbiotic relationship with zooxanthellae algae. Polyps provide these single-celled algae with shelter and nutrients. In return, zooxanthellae supply the

polyps with enough food to build reefs. Without this symbiosis, coral reefs could not exist. Coral reefs also interact with other ecosystems such as mangroves and seagrass. These interactions increase the health and diversity of all the ecosystems involved. For example, mangroves and seagrass provide nursery habitat for many coral reef fish, and also catch sediment that might otherwise smother a reef. In return, coral reefs shelter these ecosystems from erosion.[5]

These exchanges of nutrients have certain characteristics (Baumeister, 2014). First, there must be a net benefit for each partner which fosters a reinforcing feedback loop. Second, the value of the exchange is of different resources or services. Third, the benefit is something each partner can readily provide to the other. And fourth, partners respond and adapt to each other and to changing contexts. Mutualistic relationships can help buffer partners against extreme conditions, open new niches for both partners, and amplify the baseline of resource acquisition.

"In a system of increasingly interdependent parts, everything is related to every other, dependent on every other for its very definition. Lines of relationship are drawn from everywhere to everywhere. … Through individuation, it becomes more drawn into a larger whole. … Ultimately, parts join as pieces of a larger whole and find that in serving the whole, they serve themselves best" (Kiuchi & Shireman, 2002 p. 70.).

Today's leaders have found that specialization in the workforce is necessary as their industry became more complex. Specialization led to diversification, which created increasing complex organizations. Specialization requires the entire system to thrive for the specialty to thrive. This complexity has begun to shift organizations from ones structured on silos to growing interdependence. Once interdependence arrives in an organization (whether one sees it or not), the connectivity drives the need to cooperate because people who specialize need the whole to remain healthy and strong for their needs to be met. When an organization becomes conscious of this relationship it leads to the emergence of a new type of synergy and creates a new platform of evolution for the organization.

[5] https://web.stanford.edu/group/microdocs/species.html

How does nature's lesson "to reward cooperation" help us to think differently about leadership?

Creating conditions for cooperation is necessary in an interdependent complex system. As living systems evolve they become even more cooperative. Once we shift our worldview to seeing our organizations as living systems, then we can begin to see that generous organizations also behave more like dynamic networks rather than traditional hierarchies. We can also understand how all the people in our living organization are connected to each other. Given this shift, our practice of leadership would be more powerful if we assumed interdependence and did everything we could to create a system that rewards cooperation and let go of certain limiting behaviors and mindsets to make collaboration easier.

1. We need to articulate the shared higher purpose of the organization.

I have already talked about the importance of shared higher purpose in the section on *nature runs on sunlight* (Chapter Two) and its connection to releasing positive energy in an organization. I have also talked about this in *form following function* (Chapter Four) to reinforce the purpose (function) of an organization so it can become more adaptive. Shared purpose also shows up in this chapter on rewarding cooperation. Conditions that are conducive to cooperation start with employees who understand what connects them. Shared purpose is one way to support a predisposition to collaborate.

When I work with leadership teams, I ask them to identify how their colleagues help and hinder their ability to do their work. This simple exercise is a wonderful way to help teams see their interdependence. It is usually easy for an individual to identify how others hinder their work, but not as clear to understand how they (or their staff) hinder others on their leadership team. When a team realizes that they have an interdependent relationship, they are ready to be more forthright about understanding and developing their shared purpose. I believe that a team or organization's purpose comes from a deep need that they are here to meet in the world. Once that need is articulated, the purpose flows from that. First comes interdependence and second comes shared purpose.

We need to let go of hidden agendas. Hidden agendas are just that. They are motives or objectives that are not transparent to others and are manipulated to gain a particular outcome that someone wants. People who hold hidden agendas cannot be trusting or trustworthy. They don't reveal what they are thinking, and they use what others are saying, often out of context, to manipulate the group to achieve their agenda. This behavior erodes trust and integrative power. It also makes collaboration more time consuming and difficult and as a byproduct, results in more conflicts and ineffective outcomes.

I believe people in organizations are becoming more sensitive to hidden agendas and inauthenticity. As behavior and communication become more transparent, it is easier to be called out if we say one thing to one group and another to a different group. Eventually, the inconsistencies of behavior will come to light.

We need to let go of single agendas. People who hold and push for single agendas are only interested promoting their individual perspective of what matters in the organization. They may think they are wise and well-meaning, but they often do not see the complexity of the organization or how the multilayers of efforts are interconnected to the larger purpose of the organization. People who hold single agendas only collaborate with people who agree with their agenda. If people don't agree, they engage in group dynamics that waste time and block progress. They do not take the time to seek a diversity of opinions and be authentically open to alternatives or more holistic solutions. In the end, people with single agendas are perceived as difficult to work with because they never compromise, even if their lack of cooperation hurts the organization and by extension themselves.

We need to let go of our focus on self-interest. A culture of self-interest has long misquoted Charles Darwin as saying, "survival of the fittest." Rather, he said "survival of the best fit" which takes it in a different direction. One of the ways to fit best into a place and thrive for the long haul is to be sensitive to the context and form of mutually-beneficial relationships (Hutchins, 2014; Kohn, 1992). Researchers have found that mutual aid and support are found in nature and there is a strong predisposition to cooperate as such actions are closely tied to the resilience and health of the organism and the living system in which it resides.

Yet, in human organizations, self-interest and competition often has ruled the day. The message of how competing, achieving, and furthering our own self-interest brings success, permeates our organizations and society. In nature and our organizations, there are competitive relationships such as between bull elk fighting over a female cow elk, perhaps similar to how Coke and Pepsi fight over the same customers for a very similar value proposition to the customer. Competitive relationships always fall apart. And they are costly to maintain, just look at the marketing budgets of Coke and Pepsi or the toll a bull elk fight takes on both the winner and the loser with an expenditure of energy and sustaining injury.

Unfortunately, this self-interest has been used to justify actions and behaviors that create and fuel consumptive organizations (ones that take the most from their environment and do not add anything back). The fiscal crisis in 2008 is an example of where individual self-interest was used to justify actions, such as banks selling off bad housing loans and derivatives that nearly took down the global economy.

We need to replace narrow self-interest with enlightened self-interest. Enlightened self-interest was a concept that Alexis de Tocqueville discussed in his work Democracy in America (1952). In his journeys around our country, he found that Americans voluntarily joined associations to further the interests of the group and along the way served their own interests. He believed that this was what made our country unique and was its greatest potential and promise.

This dynamic is exactly what we find in nature. That by serving the whole, we also serve ourselves. We need to name how self-interest and competition shows up in our organization and replace it with the understanding that cooperation is a stronger imperative and is more adaptive and effective in a knowledge era where cooperation expands and accelerates the development of new knowledge (Halal, 1998).

2. We need to build integrative power.

Integrative power is beyond the traditional *power over* others (Brown 1986). It is built on trust and transparency, it is *power with*. It exists where people are predisposed to trust and collaborate (Banathy, 1993). Earlier we discussed three forms of organizational photosynthesis— authentic relationships, shared higher purpose, and reciprocity. These qualities in our organizational relationships help us to release positive human energy that is an extraordinary resource to achieve our mission. These ways of relating to each other also build integrative power. This kind of power is an infinite resource to an organization. Making the shift from power over to power with and seeing power as a building capacity helps create integrative power.

We need to let go of the belief that getting the largest piece of the pie is the mark of a good leader. This particular belief reflects a scarcity mindset, where power is finite and must be guarded and wielded in such a way that it adds to its own power base. In contrast, if we see power as infinite instead of finite, we realized that the more we give it away the more it comes back to us in different forms (Hagberg, 1984).

When I first started managing a department, I was anxious to learn the rules of what made a good manager. One of the lessons I learned at budget time was that my staff saw my ability to gain resources for my department as a sign I was a good manager or leader. What they and I didn't understand was that if everyone successfully draws down the maximum amount of support for their individual department, the amount that is left to support the whole is insufficient to help the organization thrive.

When I became a vice president of a college in the 1990s, our cabinet challenged this belief by articulating what our purpose was as a collective leadership team. We realized that our highest purpose was to fiercely defend the future of the institution. This may seem like extreme language, but it helped all the vice presidents to see their roles in a new way. Instead of protecting our allocations as a primary lens, we became aware that we needed to ensure that the larger mission of the college was receiving the resources it needed to thrive. This resulted in some divisions delaying their own needs while another division got what was needed to move the college forward. Our budget allocations became aligned with our higher purpose.

3. We need to design policies and systems to enhance intrinsic responsibility.

Donella Medows, a highly-regarded systems thinker, introduced the term intrinsic responsibility (2008). Intrinsic responsibility means that the system is designed to send feedback about the consequences of decisions directly, quickly, and compellingly to the decision-makers. For instance, on an individual level, a Fitbit gives feedback on eating and exercise habits. This feedback can be used to reinforce or dampen down a person's behavior. On an organizational level, this could mean that all companies that emit wastewater into a stream must place their intake pipe downstream from their outflow pipe. With this placement, there is a direct, obvious and personal outcome to the company's actions. If they continue to pollute, they will be harmed, and they will be directly responsible for the harm. The idea behind locating the place in the system where intrinsic responsibility resides helps us sharpen our feedback loops and creates a dynamic where individuals and organizations adapt their behavior to help the overall system achieve its goals.

John McKnight and his Asset Based Community Development Institute have been experimenting with a concept called *working the gap*.[6] The gap in this case is the space between an institution and a community or an organization and an individual. Sometimes our institutions act with good intentions, but the result is that the communities or individuals they work with become dependent on the institutions rather than learning, growing, and becoming more capable of solving their own problems. In an organization, we sometimes shield employees from the consequences of their choices, but this can hinder their ability to learn and evolve into more effective human beings and employees. Working the gap is a way of understanding this dynamic and examining how much and in what way a supervisor should intervene between an organization and the individual. And if leaders act, to do it in a way that does not diminish the intrinsic responsibility of the individual to become more capable and responsible.

---

[6] http://www.abcdinstitute.org/

Foundations often struggle with this dynamic. If they see themselves as an instant cash machine, over time the organizations they fund can become dependent on their grants. Working the gap suggests that foundations could focus on strengthening the local control and agency of those they fund. One way might be to require that any funds that are received are matched in some way by the grantees, so they demonstrate their strengths and commitment to the work beyond writing a grant request. In other words, make sure each group has "skin in the game." Another way is to recognize the strengths of the programs they fund, trusting that they have a better sense of the needs and the efforts that can make a difference as opposed to asking them to reshape their work in a way that reproduces "best practices" of what others have done, but might not fit their local circumstances and expertise. This behavior unintentionally diminishes the intrinsic responsibility of the people who are implementing the work. In essence, this is like the companies above who position the outflow/intake valves such that they get both the benefit and the intrinsic responsibility of their actions.

> *Mutualistic relationships in nature are those that find a benefit to all organisms involved. Generous organizations could benefit from doing the same.*

We need to learn to let go of our tolerance for large egos. We all have egos; however some individuals have large egos that command all the limelight in a room and diminish other individuals' perspectives that are necessary for a good collaborative outcome. Large egos also diminish the intrinsic responsibility of others in the organization. The large egos like to take credit for everything. They also like to accumulate personal loyalty in their relationships instead of reinforcing allegiance to the mission or larger purpose.

I once worked with an organization that had a CEO with a large ego. Over time his ego seemed to supersede the mission of the organization. Thus, the organization hired the next CEO with the awareness that they didn't want to risk the mission by hiring another large ego. In fact, they went further and started to use appropriate modesty as a criterion for hiring staff. As a result, the people in the organization have a reputation for listening, working together, and being mission focused.

4. We need to create reward systems that reinforce collaboration.

In the 1980's at the height of management by objectives, the assumption was that an individual could predict what goals would be accomplished by him or her and by what date. Now we are aware that accomplishing goals needs the input and actions of many people in an organization and we need the active support of others to accomplish our individual goals.

These days, I believe that there are many more people in our organizations that have shifted to working more collaboratively. Employees that are working in technology fields often are more predisposed to work collaboratively due to the experience of connectedness that technology creates in people's lives. Can you imagine a staff person working on social media applications not thinking in networks? These generous organizations tend to reinforce collaboration thereby optimizing the talents and energy of their staff.

Giant redwoods have a wide but shallow root system that supports trees well over 200 feet tall. As each individual tree strives toward its goal of growing toward the sun, the nearby trees intertwine their roots to create a strong root mat and their branches touch to support each other in high winds. The grandeur of a giant redwood comes from all the trees, not just the sole endeavor of a single tree.

To help shift an organizational culture from separation and individualism to interdependence and connection, we need to focus on where collaboration is already occurring and lift it up as an example of the way to do things. We also need to create ways that each individual and department can work together to create a strong network of support for all the efforts taking place in the organization—to create the strong root mat for the organization. Further, we need to learn from the collaborations that are working to see how the techniques can be spread to the rest of the organization.

Human resources systems are very influential at shaping organizational culture. Currently HR creates job descriptions, performance reviews, selection, salaries and benefits, and orientation. Each of these processes can strengthen or weaken cooperation. In addition, if we built salary adjustments around team performance and cooperation it would create intrinsic responsibility with tight feedback loops that could enhance team integration and cooperation. If our performance reviews gave deliberate feedback on cooperation, emotional intelligence, and relationship competence, they would create a distinct set of reinforcing and balancing feedback to our employees.

We need to let go of our assumptions that collaboration is time consuming, frustrating and fruitless. While collaboration can be difficult, often hidden and single agendas and large egos are a major source of the problem. Some of our systems reinforce individual-oriented behavior so group work can interfere with an individual's ability to do their job. Another obstacle to collaboration can be if employees are receiving mixed messages about what matters. These can cause confusion and lead to behaviors that make collaboration more time consuming.

Organizations which are migrating from a silo structure to an interdependent and integrated one, usually go through a phase where there are a few people who hold on to the old culture. These people maintain an individualized and separated view of the organization. They hold on to their individual authority to make their own decisions without regard or awareness of how their actions hinder other parts of the organization. When others are working together, this one person can seem to have a larger impact by simply not cooperating. Eventually peers can learn to increase feedback to that individual that their behavior is negatively impacting the organization. This feedback eventually gets louder until the person either shifts their behavior or leaves because they don't fit the system any longer.

When we shift our organization's culture to reward cooperation, collaboration becomes easier. Identifying and discussing examples of both collaboration and divisiveness and learning from them can accelerate this process. These things can take time, but as they are done, the culture begins to change so in the future there is less resistance to working toward collaboration.

5. We need to encourage trust and trustworthiness.

Trust is a precondition for cooperation. There are two sides to trust—trusting and trustworthiness (Johnson & Johnson, 1982). By trusting, we mean that we are open to sharing information, ideas, thoughts, feelings and reactions with others. We trust we will not get burnt by being open and sharing our thoughts and resources with our colleagues.

When we are trustworthy, it means that we accept, support and bring cooperative intentions to the relationship. Such acceptance communicates that we respect the people we work with and recognize their gifts and strengths. Cooperative intentions are seen in the expectations that we will all behave cooperatively with others. Trusting and trustworthiness are essential in creating conditions of cooperation in your organization.

We need to let go of being ruled by the emotions of scarcity and fear. The emotions of scarcity and fear hinder trust and trustworthiness. I was in a meeting recently and a participant shared this insight. We were talking about the future of cities and how people would need to evolve to adapt to what was coming. He mentioned three changes in how we think and behave that could accelerate the evolution of human beings. The first was to let go of fear as a primary lens to see what is happening. The second was to shift our perspective from separation and isolation to interdependence and connection. The third was to shift our perspective from scarcity to abundance.

When we view what is happening through a lens of fear, we resist what is being said and close our minds to possibilities. Everything becomes a threat. When we see ourselves as isolated or separate, we feel we must defend and protect ourselves because no one else will. When we see things through a scarcity lens, we must hold on to what we have even if it no longer is needed. Scarcity is also a great rationalization for taking more than our fair share, in case we might need it at some time in the future. We need to learn to live beyond these lenses. We need to see our connections and believe that others will support us if we let them.

We also need to move beyond fear and live a life filled with hope. Without hope, there is no reason to change the present. With hope, we can see what is missing in our present and act in a way that creates a better future (Macy & Johnstone, 2012). When we embrace abundance, we can let go of "stuff" and look at what we need and distinguish our needs from our wants. We can live more simply and richly at the same time. This is the essence of a generous organization.

The summary below shows how our focus would shift, what assumptions we would let go of, if we used nature's principle to "reward cooperation" and applied it to our organizations.

What do we need to focus on as leaders? What do we need to let go of?

1. We need to articulate the shared higher purpose of the organization.
   - *We need to let go of hidden agendas.*
   - *We need to let go of single agendas.*
   - *We need to let go of our focus on self-interest.*
2. We need to build integrative power.
   - *We need to let go of the belief that getting the largest piece of the pie is the mark of a good leader.*
3. We need to design policies and systems to enhance intrinsic responsibility.
   - *We need to learn to let go of our tolerance for large egos.*
4. We need to create reward systems that reinforce collaboration.
   - *We to let go of our assumptions that collaboration is time consuming, frustrating and fruitless.*
5. We need to encourage trust and trustworthiness.
   - *We need to let go of being ruled by the emotions of scarcity and fear.*

Questions to Consider:

As organizations become more complex, they move from generalists to specialists. This brings more complexity to our organizations. Generalists can usually provide for themselves. However, the more we specialize the more we need others to help us get the "nutrients" we need to feed ourselves. Thus, complexity brings specialization and specialization requires cooperation with others to help serve our own areas. Nature rewards cooperation through the development of mutualistic relationships. Here are some topics that could be used as reflective conversation starters with a team or a working group.

- *What if we shifted our world view to one that recognized our connection and interdependence (a natural result of increasing complexity); what would we see and how would our thinking change?*
- *Can anyone succeed over time if another fails in an interdependent system?*
- *What if the way we can serve ourselves best is to ensure that the larger systems thrives and remains healthy?*
- *What conditions are needed in our organizations and communities that are conducive to cooperation and what structures, assumptions, and processes are hindering cooperation?*
- *What feedback systems must be in place that reward cooperation in interdependent systems to help it thrive?*
- *What would our organizations look like if we achieved this kind of generous system, where individuals contributed more nutrients than they consumed for the benefit of the entire "organizational" ecosystem?*
- *What if our primary job was to help others succeed?*
- *What are innovative ways of collaborating that only take the energy it needs?*

CHAPTER SIX

Nature Banks
On Diversity

Nature is designed to create conditions conducive to life. Diversity is an important feature of these conditions. In nature, diversity equals choice and choice equals resilience of the system (Kiuchi & Shireman, 2002). If one species dies out, there is another one that can provide a similar function so the whole networked ecology can continue to thrive. One of the differences between Type I (corn field), Type II (grassland) and Type III (prairie) ecologies is the level of diversity and complexity.

Except for some weeds that might find their way into the field, the corn field is a monoculture, a Type I ecology. The corn depends on the soil for its nutrients, but adds nothing in return and so demands a huge investment in time, energy and resources. Farmers buy seed and fertilizer (enriching and depleting the soil), apply chemical herbicides to kill weeds and insects, and irrigate their crops.

As a monoculture, a corn field is particularly vulnerable to insects. There is a chemical lock and key signature between a pest and the food it seeks. Plants have ways to build their immune system which leaves traces of a "chemical signature." But this signature also makes it vulnerable to insects which are on the lookout for them. Let's say a pest, a locust, is hungry and comes upon a corn field, it sends out a signal looking for food and detects the corn's chemical signature. With thousands of corn plants, the chemical signature is very strong, and he invites his friends down for a feast.

As monoculture evolves to grassland and then evolves into a prairie, it moves from a single species to becoming more and more diverse. This diversity allows for multiple ways that nutrients can be exchanged making the entire system more resilient. For example, when the roots from one plant die back in the fall they provide nitrogen for other plants. While there is food for insects it is hidden in the diversity of the plants, there are many different plants sending out different chemical signatures which serve to hide the specific signatures of any individual plants. And even if the pest should find the plant they seek, they only wipe out the one species, not the whole prairie.

I used to work in southwestern Minnesota and saw how the farmers were intent weather watchers. They depended on the sun and rain to help their crops grow, and worried about harsh weather that could damage the crop. If a tornado or hail storm hit in the summer, it could severely damage the corn—possibly wiping out the entire crop. In addition, corn does not have a complex root system and there aren't other plants to help retain excess water, so a deluge of rain can become a runoff damaging the entire field. But in a prairie if hail wipes out the blooming plants in June, there are a series of other plants that will mature over the rest of the summer and into the fall. This ensures that there are always plants in a variety of growth stages. In addition, the plants that grow in prairies have both shallow and deep roots, so they can absorb all the rain that falls on them. If there is a small amount of rain, the shallow roots take it in. If there is a deluge, the shallow roots become saturated and the deeper root systems take over and draw the rain deeper into the soil. The diversity ensures that even a hail storm isn't catastrophic for the prairie; it can absorb massive disturbance and still maintain function. These living systems are highly resilient in part because they "bank on diversity" (Collins, 2014; Walker & Salt, 2012).

The other lesson that nature can teach us about diversity is found in the nature's structural designs. Nature is not a hierarchy with compartmentalized departments. There are no CEOs issuing commands and controlling all the species and plant life. The structure of nature's network, the connections, and the interdependencies allow the living system to self-regulate, adapt to changing conditions, and evolve to survive. As nature evolves, species and plant life begin to specialize and develop niches for themselves. However, as they specialize, they also become more dependent on other species in their ecosystem to provide nutrients that they need to thrive. These interdependencies create a predisposition to create relationships between distinct species and plant life to leverage the diversity in the ecosystem. These networks of relationships require diverse perspectives to be aware of its many parts, how they work together, and to understand its relationship with the external environment.

In order to change the way a system is working and flowing, you must first define and understand the parts of the system – name the centerpiece, determine which elements or key pieces affect or are affected by the other pieces of the system. …. (The) more detailed your system understanding becomes (by finding all the elements, ties, interconnectedness, and relationships); the more you can see the "whole picture" and increase your chances of being able to effectively adjust the system variables (Baumeister, 2014, p. 22-23).

How do these lessons from nature that "nature banks on diversity" help us think differently about leadership?

1. We need to understand how deep background assumptions work.

We need to develop the capacity to recognize the beliefs that are driving our behaviors and how they can hinder our openness to other ways of thinking. But these deep background assumptions can be hard to uncover, often, they rest below the level of consciousness. Mindfulness and reflection can help us reveal the deep assumptions we carry around within us.

We need to let go of thinking that there is only one way (and that it's ours). If we think our point of view is the only right one, we may tolerate different points of view but never fully embrace or learn from them. We need to authentically believe in the legitimacy of unfamiliar perspectives that arise out of diverse cultures, experiences and perspectives. Seeing things from a different point of view can help us open up to appreciate and learn from them.

To embrace the importance of depending on diversity in our organizations, we need to focus on our own deep background assumptions. In any paradigm shift, the beliefs and actions that helped the organization become successful in the past are not the beliefs and actions that will help the organization evolve. There must be a conscious letting go of these practices and ways of thinking to help the organization evolve.

We need to let go of the assumption that tensions are problematic. If we hold a deep background assumption that tensions are problematic, we are unlikely to create a "spacious" environment that allows the tensions of difference to co-exist. But if we have a background assumption that those tensions can provide valuable ways for us to air our differences and lead to breakthrough thinking, then we will be more open and able to welcome tensions into our teams and meetings. We will be able to invite diversity of perspective, culture, and experience into our meetings, making for richer discussions and innovative problem solving.

For example, when I was a VP at the College of St. Benedict all my direct reports were women. They didn't like conflict and would always minimize tension in our staff meetings. But I realized to get the different perspectives we needed to hear, we all needed to be comfortable with tension and invite it in, rather than trying to diminish or hide it. So we talked about how tensions can be helpful, how they could help us understand different perspective and the organization as a whole. Once we talked this through and gave everyone permission to feel okay about tensions when they were aired, we increased the effectiveness of our team.

2. We need to understand the dynamics of networks.

The need to welcome diversity is also linked to the dynamics of networks as discussed in Chapter 10. When we see our organizations as living-networked systems, we begin to see how the dynamics of networks influence the focus of our leadership. For example, we see that we can't lead from only one place within the network. We realize that the more diverse viewing points we can access within a system, the better our understanding of the dynamics of the network become.

We need to let go of our blind spots. One organization I worked with initiated a simple rule to help them respond to the dynamics of networks. They asked each staff member to look for "blind spots" in their thinking and decision-making. When staff saw a problem, they were encouraged to address it by incorporating a "loop process." It went like this: If you see a problem, it is your responsibility to take the initiative to bring people together to recommend a way to make it better. The group you informally bring together needs to represent the different perspectives and areas of the organization so any recommendation to fix the problem has been vetted by people who are close to and farther away from the problem. This practice helped the staff members see how actions in one part of the organization can have unintended consequences in another part. This process of minimizing blind spots became a part of their day-to-day practice and their organizational culture. They applied it in their organizational decision-making, in their visioning, strategic planning, communicating, and in their connections with stakeholders.

When we don't have processes that counter our blind spots, we waste the knowledge that is held in various places in our organizations or extended systems. When the attacks of 9-11 were analyzed, the FBI found that a person in the field office in Minneapolis had critical information that if it had been paid attention to might have prevented some of the attacks. The information was in the system, but we didn't have good processes to cultivate and integrate these diverse perspectives into our collective knowledge and decision-making.

The following story is another example of how knowledge exists at many different levels and how diverse perspectives can add to our collective wisdom. In Canada, natural resource managers count the caribou to ascertain the health of caribou herds during their migration. They equate the size of the herd with its health. The local indigenous population views the health of the herd from a different perspective. They look at the fat of the caribou. If there is fat on their bones it means that the caribou are storing fat for breeding, a sign that they have the resources needed to produce and maintain a healthy and growing herd. These quantitative (at a distance) and qualitative information sets are both valuable and together create a more robust understanding of the health of the caribou (Gunderson & Holling, 2002).

When I conduct culture audits in organizations, I seek out many different perspectives of the organization. This helps me see the whole living system, not just a part. As leaders, we need to focus on creating ways for diverse perspectives to be sought out and harvested.

I am often hired to coach executives who are highly skilled in traditional leadership and management. They contact me because they realize that the complexity of their organization requires a different kind of leadership than what they excel at. They are interested in pushing the boundaries of their leadership thinking and practice. They want to develop a different kind of leadership, one that brings more leadership capacity to the organization as whole. These leaders realize that they need more people in the leadership team and the organization to hold the "commons" of the organization. Without more support, the whole becomes endangered because too many people are competing for a piece of the pie without regard to the sustainability and health of the whole organization (Senge et. al., 1994).

This consulting takes the form of developing leadership teams that serve the whole organization rather than defend their part or division. We look at creating distributive leadership capacity throughout the organization to help the organization become more adaptive and the employees more engaged in serving the mission. Going through this process helps the leader recognize their own assumptions about leadership that help or hinder their ability to shape a culture where people work together to serve the highest purpose of the organization.

We need to let go of the assumption that we are separate. In a closed system, we can protect ourselves by remaining secluded and separate from the external environment. This allows us to maintain the status quo of our processes and products as well as our beliefs, behavior, and habits. But these days, we primarily have networked open systems and it is extremely difficult to keep our organization separate from the dynamics of the external environment. Our global economy reminds us daily how issues elsewhere can affect our stock prices or supply lines. Our technology and mass communications connect us across the world. We are also linked through our climate and the environment.

There is also a downside to maintaining a closed system as it isolates us from ongoing changes and distances us from our clients and customers making us vulnerable to changes in the marketplace. In nature, species that isolate themselves from their environment die. It is only in connection that species thrive. As leaders of living systems, we need to help our staff members let go of the assumption that we are separate and to see, understand, and appreciate the open system we work in.

> *We need to understand how our organization is stronger and more resilient when we see the world as connected instead of separate.*

3. We need to see how we thrive on diversity.

When our organizations are filled with individuals who thrive on diversity, they are more likely to seek out each other's input and create an enriched and welcoming workplace. This builds a stronger base of institutional diversity and enhances the culture of the organization (Taylor & Wacker, 2007). One of the ways to thrive on diversity is to appreciate different perspectives.

> Appreciating different perspectives – a requirement for full understanding of networked system, has to start with our individual responses to diversity. Do we value and respect difference? Do we believe that diversity enhances and enriches our personal lives? Individuals who thrive on diversity would seek it out and actively incorporate different perspectives, experiences, and individuals into their lives and worldview. (Allen & Cherry, 2000 p. 114).

There are many benefits to experiences that bring us into relationships with people we consider the "other." In a book titled *Common Fire: Lives of Commitment in a Complex World*, the authors interviewed a hundred individuals that had contributed to the commons over the course of their lifetime (Daloz,

Keen, Keen, Parks, 1996). It turned out that each one had an experience in their childhood that helped them see that their worldview and belief system was not the only one. Their encounter with someone who was the "other" changed the way they saw the world and started them on a path to serve the common space of our communities and organizations. There are many ways that we can learn from "the other" in our work and life. For example, getting to know a disabled person can teach us about the obstacles that they face and how they adapt. It can also help us understand how we respond to constraints in our own lives. These experiences broaden our world and our worldviews.

We need to let go of the idea that diversity is inefficient. I have been reflecting on the nature of time and how the length of our time horizon shapes how we see things. If we have an abbreviated time horizon (daily, weekly, quarterly), we may see evidence that diversity is inefficient. It requires time to listen and recognize deep background assumptions. It then requires even more time to co-create new assumptions for working and communicating in our organization. In the short term, this can seem inefficient. However, what is gained by not taking the time or making these changes in the short term can hurt you in the long term. If an organization protects itself in the short term by minimizing diversity, it limits its adaptive capacity over time. Its limited perspective keeps it from generating alternative choices that will help it succeed in the long run. Diversity may create a short-term inefficiency, but in the long term, it creates a stronger future for the organization.

We need to let go of the monoculture mentality that sees diversity as a threat. The reliance of universal solutions to address all of our problems comes from the assumption that just one culture exists in our organizations (McDonough & Braungart 2002). This one culture is often defined and aligned with the people who created the organization. In the early 1900s, the people who created organizations were primarily white men. It is their worldview that was instrumental in building our organizational designs and functions, there were few if any alternative views. These unexamined assumptions about the right way to do things reflected a monoculture mentality. This may have seemed to have worked in the past, as things appeared to move smoothly and be more profitable, at least for those at the top. But such an insular culture likely missed opportunities for designs and processes that may have added to the quality and resilience of the organization. Leaders in living systems need to let go of their own monoculture mentalities and encourage others in their organization to do so as well. When we do this, we invite a broader and more integrated understanding of the complex world we live in.

When I became a vice president of student development at a women's college, I met with the vice president of the men's college that we partnered with. As part of my first meeting with him, I asked if there was anything that the staff of my division was doing that needed to be enhanced or changed. He said he wished they would stop talking about men and women and just talk about human beings. He believed that *"human beings"* was a universal term, and when my staff used the language of men and women, it disturbed his staff.

I said that there was something about his request that disturbed me. I reflected on it for a moment and said, when we apply human beings to mean everyone, I feel like my identity as a woman is lost. He sat back and said that if we talked about men and women instead of human beings, it made him feel uncomfortable because it meant that he needed to understand himself as a man separate from his identity as a human being. This began a wonderful exploration as to how we could foster the development of men and women that capitalized on the uniqueness of gender, instead of doing the same thing for both and assuming that one way would work universally.

This conversation illustrates how a monoculture mentality hinders our ability to see and understand difference. In a monoculture mentality, any deviation from the "one way" is a threat and disturbance. The staff at the men's college saw the use of "men" and "women" instead of human beings as a disturbance to the way it had always been and the underlying assumption of what was the primary or universal framework. Women from my college, did not see themselves fully represented in the language of the college's monoculture, they wanted to use different language to allow for a more diverse culture mentality.

We need to let go of the mentality that everything is working fine without diversity. One dynamic that is found in teams that have similar demographics is the ease of not needing to negotiate fundamental assumptions about how the world works. The similarity of the team (all women of a similar age for example) also leads to a sense of trust and flow in the work. These things allow the team to focus on their work with a sense of ease. Often people fear that if we diversify the team that things will change, and it will ruin the dynamics of the team. Therefore, it can be tempting to adopt the mentality that things are working fine without any diversity.

In fact, adding diversity will probably disrupt the flow of the team. There is likely to be change requiring adjustments on all sides, and some ease, for at least a time, will be lost. What we don't see is the cost, the downside of homogeneity. It limits the perspectives, experiences, insights, and observations being considered by the team. Over time, this will cost the organization as they keep designing for people like themselves, while the demographics in the country shift (Taylor & Wacker, 2000). Just as homogeneity in investing creates a significant risk in the long-term resilience of our retirement accounts, there is a similar cost to a lack of diversity in our organizations.

I worked with a board who struggled with bringing younger people onto the board. They had scheduled the board meetings to be two-days long each quarter. This helped build a sense of connection and strong relationships among board members, but the extended meetings precluded people with young families from serving on the board. The board understood that if they were serious about diversity, they would need to change the way they operated. They needed to let go of the mentality of "don't change what's working."

4. We need to encourage inclusive leadership.

The processes, forms, and structures we use in our leadership practices matter when it comes to inclusive leadership dynamics. Typically, organizations have positional leaders in key positions and everyone else is considered to be followers. Even if they use processes that invite diversity to their teams, it may not be enough to alter the organizational culture. To establish inclusive leadership dynamics means that the core philosophy of leadership and where it resides in an organization need to be examined and rethought. We need to ask: Is leadership seen as a distributive function, able to exist at all levels of the organization? Can anyone initiate actions that align with the mission of the organization? Is leadership seen as an emergent phenomenon with many individual actions throughout the organization (Allen, et. al. 1998)? These different framings of leadership help us recognize and create more inclusive cultures that unleash a diversity of talent and perspectives.

One way to do this is to map the key hubs of influence in an organization (Rebeck, 2012). Then look for influential non-positional leaders at these key hubs who are informally having an effect on decisions, engagement, resistance and support within the organization. Inviting these individuals into strategic planning, decision-making, and focused conversations can help an organization open up their discussions and elicit different perspectives.

Another way to encourage inclusive leadership is for leaders to demand participation of their staff. Usually we use the language of "buy-in" to describe the way leaders engage with their staff on decisions. The framework of a buy-in suggests that the leader is selling an idea that they want their team members to purchase. Inclusive leadership changes this to demanding participation. Staff members don't have the option to remain silent. When this request is combined with respect and trust, it elicits diverse perspectives and experiences that add value to decision-making. Asking the following questions can help shift our leadership practices.

- *Who is at the table? Does this represent the level of diversity we need to make good decisions?*
- *Whose input do we seek? Are their voices represented in our decision-making practices? Are we missing important voices/participants?*
- *How do we facilitate the expression of different perspectives in a way that strengthens shared understanding and insight?*
- *How can we stand at a place of open inquiry when different perspectives arise in our meetings?*
- *What would it look like to develop the habit to seek to understand before we react to different points of view?*

We need to let go of the assumption that conflict is to be avoided. Conflict is often seen as a threat to efficient functioning of an organization. In fact, one of the differences between leadership and management is that leadership is about change and therefore invites conflict and controversy, while management is about maintaining the status quo and harmony in order to keep things working efficiently. Earlier in my career, I saw conflict and controversy as problems and worked to keep the work environment as conflict free as possible. Eventually I realized that tensions and differences don't limit us, instead they are the source of new and valuable thinking. Now I believe that all innovation and adaptation begin with tension. Living with the tension is how a system learns and the people in it grow and develop innovative ways of working and thinking.

We need to let go of the assumption that opposition causes splits and is a threat. In traditional management theory, opposition splits and therefore needs to be isolated, overpowered, and shut down. Yet in quantum mechanics, opposition is necessary for wholeness. In networks, opposition is necessary for understanding and achieving wholeness within the network (Allen, 2012).

Creating a culture that welcomes resistance helps to keep the resistance at the surface of the organization rather than going underground. When it is at the surface, it can be recognized as helpful feedback and can be incorporated in a way that improves the product or process. By doing so, it also reinforces that such positive resistance is valued by the organization. Leaders in a generous organization use non-defensive processes to help people challenge the status quo and bring better information to the decision-making process.

I have found that using a "round robin" approach can illustrate how the organization values diverse perspectives and even opposition. In these sessions, I ask people to reflect individually on a topic that's up for discussion, then I lead a round-robin facilitation session where each person shares their thoughts, but just offering one at a time, and then we move on to the next person, going round the circle, and then we let each person offer a second thought, and so on. This gives people the time to think about what they have shared and consider the diverse perspectives they are hearing from others in the circle. It also equalizes the participation ensuring that no one dominates the conversation.

In these sessions or in other meetings, if you run into an idea that you don't understand, respond from a place of inquiry or curiosity, asking, "Tell me more about this." When you hear an idea that shocks you or makes you uncomfortable instead of responding to the idea, say, "That's interesting, tell us some more." Be sure to write each idea on the board. When people get defensive they tend to only write the ones they like. Collecting everyone's ideas, even if you don't agree with them, shows respect and often makes it easier to address them. When we are heavily siloed, any new ideas can be looked on as a potential threat. Instead we need to see tensions as promising and invite differences in so we can see the whole. When we air them, we can often find new perspectives that can lead us to see something of value.

The summary below shows how our focus would shift, what assumptions we would let go of, if we used nature's principle to "bank on diversity" and applied it to our organizations.

What do we need to focus on as leaders? What do we need to let go of?

1. We need to understand how deep background assumptions work.
- *We need to let go of the assumption that tensions are problematic.*
- *We need to let go of thinking that there is only one way (and that it's ours).*
- *We need to let go of the assumption that tensions are problematic.*

2. We need to understand the dynamics of networks.
- *We need to let go of our blind spots.*
- *We need to let go of the assumption that we are separate.*

3. We need to see how we thrive on diversity.
- *We need to let go of the idea that diversity is inefficient.*
- *We need to let go of the monoculture mentality that sees diversity as a threat.*
- *We need to let go of the mentality that everything is working fine without diversity.*

4. We need to encourage inclusive leadership.
- *We need to let go of the assumption that conflict is to be avoided.*
- *We need to let go of the assumption that opposition causes splits and is a threat.*

Questions to Consider:

What is the innate value of diversity in an interdependent system? Nature banks on diversity because it is designed to see diversity as a critical lynchpin to its goal to create conditions for life to thrive into the future. And yet many of our organizations are still struggling to see and articulate the innate value of diversity in their organization.

What is the risk in homogeneity? This is a provocative question designed to help us examine the cost of too much homogeneity in our organizations or communities. Nature banks on diversity because too much homogeneity does not allow the ecological system to thrive. What if this was true in our own organizations but because we were focused on the short term, we can't see the threat embedded in homogeneity over time?

From these provocative questions arise leadership questions: What if we believed that we need to bank on diversity for the future sustainability of our organizations. These ideas and questions could be used to assess how the organization is currently banking on diversity to help it evolve and maintain its resilience.

- *How do decision-making processes help or hinder the unleashing of diverse thinking, perspectives, and ethnicities in our organization?*
- *How do leaders make meaning of the value of diversity in organizations?*
- *What do networks have to teach us about the value of diversity?*
- *What if diversity is necessary for wholeness?*
- *Do we value and respect difference?*
- *Do we believe that diversity enhances and enriches our personal lives?*
- *Individuals who thrive on diversity would seek it out and actively incorporate different perspectives, experiences, and individuals into their lives and worldview.*
- *What would our organizations look like if we designed diversity into them?*

CHAPTER SEVEN

Nature Curbs Excess From Within

Nature's overall purpose is to create conditions conducive for life on this planet, now and in the future. It uses feedback loops to determine whether something helps life to thrive and if it helps the ecosystem maintain a dynamic equilibrium that facilitates that end.

In nature, there are two types of feedback loops, reinforcing and balancing. Reinforcing feedback loops encourage an increase in a specific type of behavior and primarily represents growth. This is a straightforward positive loop. If something has been successful, then it is logical to keep doing more of the same.

The story of ants searching for food is an illustration of a reinforcing feedback loop. One core purpose (function) of ants is to acquire food/nourishment for the colony. A great deal of food must be found to feed a growing colony. But you probably haven't noticed many single ants bringing food back to the colony. It typically takes a lengthy line or mass of ants before we notice them. But the mass of ants bringing food back starts with just one ant dropping a pheromone trail.

As this first ant searches for food it drops a weak chemical trail of pheromones along the way. Once it finds food, it returns to the colony on the same trail, dropping another layer of pheromones, thus strengthening the trail. With two layers of pheromone, other ants are more attracted to follow it. Each additional ant that follows the trail to the food and returns, drops additional pheromones along the way. Through these actions, the trail gets stronger and stronger creating a robust feedback loop. As more ants follow the trail, more are attracted to it and soon most of the colony's foraging resources (ants) are spending all their time following this trail and directly supporting the colony's purpose—to survive and thrive. Through positive feedback loops, the trail is a form that fits the function of gathering enough food for the ant colony.

If a branch falls and blocks the trail, the ants find a way around or over it, reestablishing the chemical trail and the function of the trail for gathering food. We see similar dynamics on our freeways. Have you ever been behind a car that is driving below the speed limit in the fast lane? First there is a backup of cars, and then a car shifts over to the right lane and goes around the slow car on the left. One after another, the other cars do the same thing. The function of the highway is to get the drivers from one place to another. When there is an obstruction, drivers find a way around the obstruction. Their form shifts to adapt to the feedback about the conditions, so the function of getting to work or visiting family and friends can be met.

Reinforcing loops need balancing loops to keep living systems in balance. A balancing feedback loop creates a correction that curbs excess. The predator-prey relationships in nature illustrate both reinforcing and balancing feedback loops. The deer population rises when food is plentiful, which is a reinforcing loop. As the deer population increases, predators (such as wolves) increase preying on the deer. This cuts back the deer population, which eventually leads to a decrease in the wolf population—balancing loops. The rise and fall of animal populations continue over time creating a dynamic equilibrium in nature.

While it is tempting to see nature as benign, if a system is very out of equilibrium, the balancing loop can seem destructive. The threat of forest fires can increase if there is a lot of deadfall in the forest. The forest fire that occurs because of this excess deadfall is initially destructive to the forest. However, nature also designs trees to leave seed pods that only open under intense heat, thereby, creating the means for the next generation of trees to germinate.

We need both reinforcing and balancing loops in our organizations. For example, we might reinforce a successful way of making money such as manufacturing more and more widgets, but if we do not balance it out by ensuring that our resources are plentiful, our supply line can continue to make the product, our customers will continue to buy, our employees have the hours, energy and resources to do the work, and our local communities are healthy and strong—we do not have a successful, sustainable system.

Nature's feedback loops occur in *cycles and in cyclical processes* that can help balance and reinforce certain behaviors. These cyclical processes, like changes in the seasons, can be used to transition feedback loops from reinforcing to balancing. For example, different seasons reinforce or balance various aspects of an ecosystem. I live in Minnesota, where fall and winter help to dampen down certain pests that might thrive in the summer but can't make it through the winter.

Nature's purpose is to support future generations of life which requires a long view. However, to achieve that purpose, distinct feedback loops must operate in both the short and long term. The time horizon is directly connected to the variety of feedback loops that are in play. Climate change is an example of the need for a longer point of view, and yet there are also feedback loops that are creating short-term changes, such as adaptations in the migration patterns of animals.

Although we may not be conscious of them, organizations also have cyclical processes that create a dynamic equilibrium that curbs excess. Contract renewals, performance reviews, budget development, annual stockholder meetings are examples of annual cyclical processes that exist in organizations. Strategic planning cycles are also a longer-term cyclical process. We also have regular staff meetings that can be a more rapid cyclical process to balance or adjust reinforcing loops. With consciousness, we can use these cycles, like nature, to intentionally curb excess.

The idea that the dynamics of a system can help it regulate itself is a powerful one. It is very different from the current norm in our organizations where we use outside forces to curb our excesses. We go about our business until governmental regulations or the legal system steps in. While these regulations were created to diminish harm to people, many organizations complain about the waste of time and energy that goes along with meeting these standards. We often portray them as burdensome and resist, often creating greater problems for the organization itself as well as adding to the time and cost of the issue.

> *What if government regulations were seen as a helpful feedback loop,*
> *giving us useful information about our product or a process we use?*

What if we designed our system like nature does, where we wouldn't need outside regulations because we would generate our own controls and self-regulate our actions from within our organization?

How does Nature's lesson to "to use feedback to curb our excess" inspire us to think differently about leadership?

Typically, we don't see our organizations as living systems, therefore, sustainability, if it is a goal, is engineered and requires supervision. However, if we did see our organizations as living systems, we would value the long view and would optimize the feedback loops that would help it evolve to be sustainable on its own.

Consumptive organizations aren't evolved enough to consider sustainability as an integral part of their existence. This not only makes them less sustainable, it leads to costs in the short term as well. For example, there is a cost when these organizations view the earth's or their customer's resources as unlimited. With this attitude, they are unlikely to seek low-energy, long-term solutions to human and material problems, nor to make other adjustments as needed. As we evolve our consumptive organizations toward generous systems, our organizing intent shifts from consumption to sustainability and we make adjustments in our attitudes and behaviors.

1. We need to use feedback loops and other tools to curb excesses.

Nature does not act as if excess is normal and should be tolerated. While there is temporary excess, nature uses feedback loops and cyclical processes to continually bring the system back into dynamic equilibrium. So, if one living system, nature, can do this, surely our human living organizations can learn to do the same. As systems evolve, there are times when we need to let go of beliefs and actions that served us well earlier in the life of the organization (Land, 1986). Leaders in living systems need to surface beliefs that no longer serve the organization. We also need to make sure that the balancing feedback loops in our organizations are strong enough to curb this behavior.

> *In nature, balancing or reinforcing loops happen naturally,*
> *whereas we must intentionally design them into our systems.*

To become a generous organization, we need to establish feedback loops to curb our excesses. But first we need to identify the excesses and understand their costs.

We need to let go of our tolerance for excess. Our organizations run on a set of beliefs that both serve and hinder our work. Part of the reason we tolerate excess is that we believe it is the natural state of things and therefore largely unchangeable. There are so many instances of organizational excess; we sometimes forget that we have any other options. We become numb to the behavior and its impact on the organization's bottom line and the people in the organization. For instance, we are so used to wasting time that we don't aspire to become better at how we utilize our time and energy. We shrug when we learn how much some CEOs are making and how out of proportion it is to other compensation in the organization. We tolerate abuses of power by people in a variety of positions in the organization, not just at the top. We tolerate how we consume the energy of human beings in our organization. We tolerate people who have egos that hinder the work. And we tolerate an excess of problematic behavior.

For example, I recently conducted an organizational culture audit which revealed that many employees did not trust leadership team members because they often violated confidentiality. Up until the audit, the feedback loop available to individuals in this organization was just their own observations. It was one-way feedback and it taught them not to trust the team. When I named this dynamic in a report to the interviewees, it became "known" in the organization and opened the opportunity for a public conversation. The feedback loop transformed from an individual observation to an organizational dialogue. It took courage and openness for the leadership team to allow this feedback to take place. They cared about their organization's success and wanted to do the right thing. They chose to act on this feedback by apologizing and taking responsibility for their actions, an important first step toward increasing trust. Their ongoing actions will create feedback through which employees can determine whether the leadership team can continue to earn back their trust.

We need to identify the excesses that plague our organizations. In Chapter Three, we discussed many of the "wastes" of an organization. Here are a few more that show up as excesses: There is often an excess of *meaningless tasks* filling our organizations, but we don't have the feedback loops to understand how destructive they are or how to stop the spread of them. There is an *excess of data* that can overwhelm or distract us. To be effective organizations need to identify what data makes a difference and how to transform it into usable knowledge and wisdom. Sometimes when people are placed in leadership positions, they use their power to control others, rather than support their work and efforts. This creates an *excess of challenges* that hinder the accomplishment of the mission. If you go into an organization many people will be able to name who is using an *excess of power* and how it is negatively impacting their ability to get their work done. Usually the person's supervisor is expected to be or activate a balancing loop. However, often the supervisor either doesn't realize how problematic their direct report is or is reluctant to get involved.

As discussed earlier, we have *excesses of meetings that consume human energy*. Often our default mode is to address all efforts, issues, and problems through meetings and committees. Yet, our meetings and committees create a huge burden of "organizational time" on employees and takes away from the time they must spend performing their job responsibilities. Sometimes we have an *excess of ego and self-interest or problematic behavior* in our organizations. In some instances, the organization has feedback loops that curb this behavior and in other instances, these behaviors are rewarded with attention. For some even negative attention is seen as recognition of them or their ideas, which creates a reinforcing feedback loop and increases this behavior.

There are also examples of excess *greed* in our organizations. A driving reinforcing loop in organizations is often to make more money, to be more profitable. While this makes sense on some level, it can also create a distorted focus on making money at the exclusion of all else. This greed can have unintended consequences of negatively impacting the long-term growth of the company or even the entire sector. The financial industry demonstrated this with the economic meltdown in 2008. Focusing on money instead of meaning has been shown to cause businesses to grow more slowly than organizations that focus on customers' well-being and satisfaction or have a purpose driven culture that takes the long view (McLeod, 2016).

We need to let of the assumption that executives drive the performance of our organization. In a living system that is interdependent, no one individual is solely responsible for the performance of the organization. It takes many people working together to realize a successful organization. Yet, we have many examples of excess compensation, where CEO's are compensated in geometrically higher proportion than their employees. This model of compensation has created a strong reinforcing loop for top executives, without the needed balancing loops to curb, slow down, or correct the excess of this compensation model.

2. We need to focus on the long-time horizon.

When we think about our organization's success or achievements in short-time horizons, it leads us to focus on short-term feedback loops. The difficulty with this is that things that work in the short term don't always succeed in the long term (Wahl, 2016). For example, using cheap oil and burning fossil fuels were strategies that generated short-term profits (even if the short term was 100 years). However, it is becoming apparent that these choices have led to climate change that threatens the world and the people in it. Currently fracking is a strategy used across the country to sustain cheap energy in oil. Yet, seen over the long term, it may threaten the quality of ground water in nearby communities.

Seventh generation thinking invites us into a long-time horizon. This philosophy comes from the Constitution of the Iroquois Nation (Vecesy & Venables, 1980). It states, "In every deliberation, we must consider the impact on the seventh generation… even if it requires having skin as thick as the bark of a pine." (pp 173-174). It assumes that the way we solved problems in the past have shaped our current challenges and the way we solve them today will have consequences for future generations. To put this idea to use, we must place ourselves in the fourth generation and then make decisions based on what we have learned from decisions made three generations ago and how it may impact people three generations in the future.

Keep in mind a long-time horizon influences what we pay attention to. Recently, I talked to a mayor of a suburban city outside of Minneapolis. She was talking about her city's water needs for the future. Since her city is landlocked, she was thinking about how her city could capture and use water more effectively. If she was a typical politician, she would be making decisions based on her election cycle. But her long-time horizon led her to look farther and raise issues that will impact her city in the long run, not the next two years. It is likely that in doing so, she will come up with answers, or perhaps more questions, that will enable the city to be more successful in the water plans they do end up creating.

Long-time horizons invite more data and feedback loops and help to create a better understanding of the various consequences of our actions, all important to our decision-making process. As leaders, we need to push out our own time horizon and do the same for our organizations.

We need to let go of the more (today) is better mentality. Many organizations have created reinforcing feedback loops centered on increasing the profits or size of their organization. But the reinforcing loops don't question if this growth is the best criteria for creating a strong company over time. This predisposition that growth is good no matter what supports excess in a system; there is no acknowledgement of the limits to growth.

There is a movement in the entrepreneur field to redefine success (Burlingham, 2005). These small giants look to sustainability, core values, and their relationships with their employees and their communities as the key measures of success. They aren't focusing just on growth; they are aspiring to be great. Borrowing from Darwin, generous sustainable living organizations must strive towards the best fit for itself in its environment.

3. We need to create intentional robust feedback systems.

All living systems have feedback systems in play. This is true for both consumptive and generous organizations. The challenge for an organization that wants to curb excess and waste is that our reinforcing feedback loops accelerate excess—which can be exciting and invigorating—yet can cost the organization valuable resources and money. On the other hand, our balancing feedback loops can seem cautious and less compelling, yet offer valuable checks to the reinforcing loops and lead to long-term health of the organization. Being intentional about our feedback systems is a way to use and strengthen the naturally occurring dynamics in an organization to benefit the living system.

To make feedback systems intentional, we first need to see them. One way to make feedback systems visible is to think about events and decisions as streams instead of distinct separate entities or actions. We need to see decisions as connected to each other, coming from the past, flowing through the present and into the future (as in the seventh generation thinking described above). If we had that perspective, we would understand that the way we made decisions in the past impact our agenda and decisions today. For example, if a leadership team's decisions in the past resulted in a decrease of trust of their leadership, gaining the active cooperation of employees for today's decisions will be more challenging. When we begin to see our actions and decisions as part of a stream of choices and actions, we also begin to see how feedback flows through our organizations.

Our organizational values can provide us a lens to search for the feedback systems that are in play in our organizations. *Core values* have a robust feedback loop in organizations. Our core values are incorporated in our mission statements, but they are often even more apparent in the decisions we make about how our organization operates in the world, the products or services we provide, and the culture within the organization. When these values are violated, the people who are breaking them quickly face consequences up to being fired (Lencioni, 2012).

Accidental values are behaviors and beliefs that are part of the culture of the organization and have significant impact on policies and decisions, though often without conscious or recognized awareness. For instance, I consulted with an organization who worked with blind people. Recognizing the needs of its clients, the organization was very attentive to where things were physically located in their offices and made sure not to make changes to the layout. Over time, the organization unconsciously took on the attitude that "keeping everything in its place" creates safety and projected this on to every program and action in the organization. This unnamed "accidental value" did not serve them well as it kept them from being able to adapt to the changing external environment.

Permission-to-play values are behaviors or beliefs that may be required to work in the organization, but they are often "unconscious givens" and are not articulated or reinforced. For example, honesty and respect are values that we seek in prospective employees. However, the organization's feedback loops may not actually reinforce these behaviors or may even dampen them down when dishonesty or disrespect occurs. We can see this when a dishonest employee is advanced within the organization.

Feedback loops are more robust when the reinforcing or balancing dynamic is transparent. The more information that is openly shared, the more people will see what is being rewarded or balanced. Sharing why a balancing action was taken helps to ensure that feedback loops are understood within an organization. These stories help people to see and experience feedback more consciously. As we make these dynamics more conscious, people will act accordingly further supporting the behavior.

Culture is defined, created, and supported by the feedback loops
that exist in our organizations.

How we behave in crisis, what gets rewarded or recognized, what gets ignored, what gets measured and controlled, and what gets people fired, are examples of how culture gets embedded in an organization and the feedback loops that exist in our organizations (Schein, 1985).

4. We need to mine feedback for helpful information.

Once we become more conscious of the feedback loops that exist in and around our living organizations, we need to take the time to make sense of the feedback. We receive feedback from both external and internal systems. The space between the organization and the outside environment can be filled with useful feedback. Yet we rarely examine this feedback for the important insights it may reveal about our organization, we don't often stop and ask, "What does this feedback mean to our products or industry?" (McDonough & Braungart, 2002, 2013)

What if the feedback showed that there is a failure in the design of a product that is having a negative impact on people's health? After hearing that their products created emissions that were harmful to people, the paint and carpet industry started to redesign their products to decrease these emissions. By so doing, the companies are being more responsible stewards of the environment and can promote the safety of their products, and thus potentially increase sales. This is an example of learning from feedback and how we are better served when we ask what it means and choose a response that is not based on defensiveness.

> *We need to pay more attention to helping our organization make meaning of the feedback loops within and between the organization and its environment.*

We can enhance the learning by closing the loops on feedback by quickly and directly responding to the issues raised, and by increasing the speed and immediacy of feedback to people in our organizations. We learn faster when we see the connection between feedback and consequences.

We need to let go of slow feedback loops. There are many reasons that individuals may want to slow or block feedback loops. Sometimes they do not feel a part of the organization and so do not feel obliged to pass on this information. Or they may feel that the feedback is coming from a source that is not credible or that the feedback may increase their work load. Other times, they may feel that the feedback reveals something negative about them or their work and do not want the feedback aired. There are many ways that individuals can slow these feedback loops. One way is not to share the feedback when they receive it or dismiss or minimize its value, such as challenging the source of the feedback in a way that persuades others to ignore the feedback.

We often have employees who are not aligned with our organization's core values, but we seldom move quickly to address this issue. Why are we slow to respond when these people behave outside of our organizational values? What slows or discounts this kind of feedback in an organization? These are questions we need to ask ourselves and team leaders. We need to pay attention to feedback, learn what is relevant, see the consequences in short and long-term time frames and act.

> *The good news is that feedback has a way of returning if it is important.*
> *The dynamics of feedback is such that if the system is out of balance,*
> *the feedback will keep returning.*

5. We need to strengthen relationships in our decision-making processes.

When we examine ideas and strategies with other individuals, teams, and customers, we reinforce ethical decision-making. By receiving feedback from multiple sources, a wider set of criteria is brought into the decisions. For example, if a strategy was developed primarily to make money, by sharing this plan with those who would be impacted by the strategy we receive information that may influence our plans. If customers are worried about the environment and the money-making strategy has a negative impact on environmental issues, this feedback may help to create a better strategy that is beneficial to the company's bottom line and the environment. To encourage conversations that provide useful feedback, our relationships need to be based in reciprocity between the seekers and givers of feedback. Reciprocity allows for authentic communication where we tell the truth to each other about the issue that is being discussed. Feedback is not always supportive or critical. But it is always useful. It helps us see the consequences of our decisions through other's eyes and their viewing point in the system. Isolation in decision-making processes hinder feedback loops from forming and being heard.

In my experience when we disregard feedback in the system, it only gets louder and harder to ignore. For example, the environment is giving us feedback in the form of climate change. Some have heard it and others haven't. Our policies and lifestyle haven't changed enough to rebalance the system. So, the feedback loops on climate just keep getting louder.

We need to let go of emotions that impede feedback. Feedback loops are interesting in part because the role emotions play in receiving feedback. To curb excess in our organizations, we need to focus on how emotions affect what we and our employees ignore or disregard in feedback. There are negative consequences when we deny feedback because we don't like what it is telling us. Yet, we often deny feedback when our emotions are engaged. We may have a rationale for why we ignore it, but under our rational explanation is our emotion. Neuroscience has found that all decisions are processed through our amygdala; the emotional memory chip of the brain (Goleman, 1995, 2002). Therefore, it would strengthen our organizations if emotional intelligence was part of our organizational culture. This would help us all see the feedback loops and work to understand what they mean without rejecting them due to the emotions we feel about the information.

6. We need to cultivate and model mindfulness.

All the areas of focus listed above require greater individual and collective mindfulness in an organization. Without the capacity to be fully present to what is occurring, we cannot see or examine our thoughts clearly (Kabot-Zinn, 1994; Carroll, 2006; Gonzalez, 2012). Mindfulness helps us manage our emotions, it helps us go deeper to see feedback loops, it helps us learn from feedback and move through any tensions and emotions that arise from the feedback that is coming at us. If we want to curb excess, we need develop our own and the organization's capacity to bring a mindful practice to our day-to-day work.

The summary below shows how our focus would shift, what assumptions we would let go of, if we used nature's principle to "use feedback to curb excess" and applied it to our organizations.

What do we need to focus on as leaders? What do we need to let go of?

1. We need to use feedback loops and other tools to curb excesses.
   - *We need to let go of our tolerance for excess.*
   - *We need to identify the excesses that plague our organizations.*
   - *We need to let of the assumption that executives drive the performance of our organization.*

2. We need to focus on the long-time horizon.
   - *We need to let go of the more (today) is better mentality.*

3. We need to create intentional robust feedback systems.

4. We need to mine the feedback for helpful information.
   - *We need to let go of slow feedback loops.*

5. We need to strengthen relationships in our decision-making processes.
   - *We need to let go of emotions that impede feedback.*

6. We need to cultivate and model mindfulness.

Questions to Consider:

Anyone who has said that their closet is too small to hold their wardrobe, or considered buying a bigger house because their kids toys have taken over the house, are experiencing the hazards of not having adequate balancing feedback loops in their lives. Nature uses reinforcing feedback loops to grow and expand a species, territory, size of the organization or budget. However, we often focus more on the growth than we do on balancing feedback loops that dampen down the growth cycle and help the system maintain dynamic equilibrium. For a closet that is too full, a balancing feedback loop would be to not get a bigger closet, but have fewer clothes. Or to give away as many clothes as you buy in a year. Positional leaders can strengthen their ability to curb excess from within their organization by reflecting and studying the strength of their balancing feedback loops. Here are some questions to ponder.

- *How can intrinsic responsibility for stewardship be embedded in an organizational culture? (i.e. have balancing loops embedded in each employee.)*
- *How can we design our organizations in such a way that it naturally curbs excess instead of depending on positional leaders (or outside regulation) to do this?*
- *How can we use nature as a model to help us redesign our organizations so the day-to-day feedback loops help us curb our various excesses?*
- *How can we recognize when feedback loops are out of balance (i.e. too much reinforcing or balancing loops) in our organization? How do we bring a consciousness to the feedback systems we are using to drive business?*
- *What if we used policy and procedure manuals as intentional balancing loops in our organizations?*
- *How can we leverage cyclical processes to help us curb excess from within our organization?*
- *Why are we slow to respond (balancing loop) when people behave outside of organizational values?*
- *What slows or discounts feedback in our organization?*

- *How can our organizations create feedback loops or cyclical processes that curb the excess of meaningless tasks in our organization?*
- *How can our organizations create feedback loops or cyclical processes that curb the excess of data in our organization?*
- *What can an organization do to stop the spread of meetings and committees so only the ones that are needed are created and that we only meet for the needed amount of time to get the job done?*
- *Where are our feedback loops that help us reduce excess of meetings and organizational time?*

CHAPTER EIGHT

Nature Depends on Local Expertise and Self-Organization

The ability to self-organize is the strongest form of system resilience. A system that can evolve can survive almost any change by changing itself.
— Donaella Meadows (2008 p. 159)

Nature is designed as a network filled with a vast interconnected web of species exchanging nutrients and recycling wastes (Callenbach, 2008). Each species in a local ecology is connected to each other and the dynamic environment they reside in, they cannot be fully understood by themselves. Each one depends on local expertise finding just the right way to evolve, building on their inner capacities and the local conditions, and supporting each other and the larger ecology. The molecular self-assembly of the albacore shell is an example of this remarkable local expertise. The albacore shell is one of the hardest surfaces per square inch found in nature. It is so tough that it can withstand the weight of a truck. It is created through combining molecules that are composed of both organic and inorganic minerals found in a mollusk's diet.

We have a lot to learn from this process of self-assembly. When humans want to create similar hard surfaces, we use heat and pressure imposed from the outside, a top-down method. By depending on local actors in an ecological system to self-organize, nature can achieve comparable results without the added "expense" of heat and pressure. In nature's design, self-organizing and local expertise trumps industrial processes (Wheatley & Kellner-Rogers, 1996).

Each of these micro-ecologies is unique, with different sets of relationships and species interaction, dependent on the local conditions. Local expertise is optimized when organisms behave in a way that allows their relationships with other species to form, change, and end as their local environment continues to shift. Nature counts on the plant and animal life in each micro-ecology to initiate action it needs to respond to changing conditions. This local adaptive expertise is revealed in how individual organisms behave and how their relationships with other species form, change, and end as needed to ensure that the living system thrives. These relationships are mutualistic, designed to have a positive benefit to each other. These relationships are also self-organizing, there is no direction from "on high" or from outside the ecology. They find and work with each other organically, becoming more together than they are apart.

For example, lichen stems from a mutualistic relationship between fungi and algae. The algae use photosynthesis to provide food for itself and to share with the fungi. The fungi provide shelter and mineral nutrients to the algae. This symbiotic, cooperative relationship makes fungi and algae together greater than the sum of their parts, surviving over time and place. The oldest known lichen is 400 million years old and 20,000 different types of lichen thrive from the polar regions to the tropics.

Another example of self-organizing comes from how bees make use of reinforcing loops to keep their hive at optimum temperature. In each hive, certain drone bees are genetically designed to flap their wings faster if the temperature in the hive rises above the optimum temperature. This creates increased ventilation and air circulation. But if the temperature continues to rise, it activates another set of drones, which have a higher set point than the original group, to join the effort. Once the temperature drops, the balancing feedback loop sends this information to the bees, and they cease flapping their wings so rapidly. The temperature and the feedback loops reinforce their behavior to help them self-organize and regulate their environment.

Nature's resilience is built on the local entity's ability and freedom to adapt and organize to serve the entire system. It is one of the reasons that nature depends on local expertise and initiative. It counts on species to understand what's needed, and then to self-organize and take action to help keep the larger ecosystem in dynamic balance. If curbing excess is about self-regulation, depending on local expertise is about self-organization. Local expertise and self-organization are tightly coupled—you can't have one without the other.

This makes nature both efficient and effective. It allows for new possibilities and adaptations that fit the needs and changes in the system. It doesn't prescribe; it unleashes the ability to self-organize. As a result, it is both creative and orderly. You could say that organizing is free in nature—another form of generosity.

What would it look like if we trusted local expertise and self-organization?

Let's imagine for a minute a world filled with people who all needed to be individually directed before acting. It would be like someone trying to keep 6-7 billion plates spinning at the same time. You can just imagine the spinner moving from plate to plate to plate, focusing on the plates that are slowing down, getting to them just before they crashed. Each one would be a crisis narrowly avoided, only minutes later to be back in crisis mode again. The spinner would quickly end up exhausted and collapsed on the floor with plates crashing all around.

One of the differences between consumptive and generous organizations is found in the mindset of the people leading them. Leaders of consumptive organizations believe that people need direction while generous organization leaders believe that people can self-organize and collectively achieve powerful results. Consumptive leaders hold the reins close at hand while leadership in a generous organization is distributed throughout the organization. When people at the top don't trust in people locally to make good decisions, they are blinded to their potential and create standardized procedures (best practices) and apply them to all situations. Consumptive organizational leaders likely believe that their approach is more effective and efficient since they have oversight and control of the work and can thus step in as needed to move things forward or redirect. It may surprise them to learn that this approach is costlier because they use more energy, time, and money to support and monitor the work.

These strict rules, processes, and policies also dampen down initiative in employees. Standardization hinders self-organization. This kind of top-down direction not only creates tensions between the positional leaders and the local employees, it often leads to inferior processes and products.

In contrast, generous organizations recognize the value of local expertise and create platforms to support self-organization and help develop and affirm people's capacity and confidence to initiate and organize their own work. They make sure that their staff feels free to use their expertise wherever they sit in the system. This creates a win-win situation as the employees feel that they have a vital role to play in the organization which makes them more likely to further contribute and stay with the organization, and the organization benefits from their insights and input.

As I write this Hurricane Harvey has been battering Houston, Texas. While there are first responders doing wonderful work, they have been overwhelmed by the requests for aid. The gap has been filled in, in part, by others who are doing what needs to be done to help each other in a very difficult situation. The stories of individuals rescuing neighbors and others endangered by the flood waters are inspiring. They also reflect the ability of human beings to self-organize.

> *What would our organizations look like if we assumed there*
> *was valuable knowledge, expertise and experience at the local level?*

Generous organizations recognize that intelligence exists at all levels and intentionally reinforce self-organization so that innovation can bubble up from all levels of the organization. Complex adaptive leadership theory acknowledges this dynamic. The role of leadership is to generate conditions for this "bottom up" advancement, such as employee initiated organizing and innovation, managing resources and strategic direction from the top (so that it encourages bottom up innovation), and facilitating the interaction between the top-down and bottom up dynamics (McKelvey & Lichtenstein, 2007).

For example, in 1948, 3M launched its 15% program to create a structure and process to encourage self-organization for innovation. They offer every employee the opportunity to use 15% of their time to pursue an interesting idea. For 3M, this has led to 22,800 patents including the famous Post-it notes (100: A Century of Innovation - 3M Innovation, 2002). Google has a 20% program that is their version of this idea and is credited with the creation of Gmail. Both programs are examples of how companies can create structures to support and tap local expertise and talent in their organizations.

Another example comes from my consulting practice. For the past six years, I have been working with the Sherwood Foundation and the Nebraska Community Foundation. The Nebraska Community Foundation has a saying: *The only people who can transform a community are the people who live, sleep, and work there.* This philosophy is an expression of their belief in the ability of rural communities to self-organize and initiate change that strengthens their locality. The two foundations partnered with each other and used this philosophy to develop an initiative to help rural Nebraska communities create local unrestricted endowments to build discretionary assets and leadership capacity. The power of this initiative is that the designers understand that the path to develop local assets should depend on the local expertise and culture of each community. In this initiative, each community is free to approach the endowment building work in a way that is distinctly their own.

How does nature's lesson to "depend on local expertise and self-organization" help us to think differently about leadership?

What should leaders focus on to encourage local expertise and self-organization? What mindsets and practices no longer serve an organization that seeks to unleash the talent throughout the organization?

1. We need to create and support self-organizing employee cultures.

Lately, more and more organizations have been experimenting with creating self-organizing systems. Zappos created systems that allow workers to manage themselves without the aid of middle managers. Agile software development processes often use rapid problem-solving and empowered teams instead of traditional hierarchies (The Wall Street Journal, August 19, 2015). Self-organizing experiments don't always work but over the last 10-15 years, many have. When they do it is often because the organizations have a light supervisory and leadership footprint that makes way for innovation and saves organizational energy and resources.

It requires a special kind of talent and leadership to grow and nurture these self-organizing employee cultures. I have worked with several organizations that are developing cultures of self-organization. In each case they seek to hire or develop employees who have four capacities:

1. They are able to be able to initiate and organize their own work and learning.
2. They are self-aware. They have a realistic assessment of their strengths and weaknesses to trigger their learning process.
3. They believe in the organization's mission and purpose and align their work to fit into and support that mission.
4. They are emotionally intelligent. They are able to manage their emotions and do not spread drama in the workplace.

Distributive leadership complements this spirit of self-organization. Distributive leadership believes that leadership can occur at any level of the organization and all individuals have capacity to be agents of leadership (Brafman & Beckstrom, 2006; Raelin, 2010; Schmitz, 2012). The same four capacities of self-organization are required to develop a culture of distributive leadership. (We also discuss distributive leadership in Chapter Nine.)

We need to let go of the assumption that the only source of intelligence rests at the top. Sometimes we act as if we believe that intelligence rises to the top of the organization and stays there. This deep background assumption shapes how we pay our leaders, who we credit with organizational success, and what leadership looks like. It also blinds us to the power of self-organization.

In **Being Digital**, Nicholas Negroponte notes that the growth of the Internet is shifting our sense of the source of intelligence (1995). For instance, we used to have a broadcast system for our entertainment. People in Hollywood would decide what programs to create and what we could watch on our TVs each night. Now with the Internet, we, not someone at a distance at the top of the broadcasting system, decide what we're interested in watching and when and how we're going to watch it. The source of the intelligence has shifted; we are led by our own inquiry.

2. We need to recognize and seek out knowledge, experience, and expertise wherever it exists.

In hierarchical organizations, there is an assumption that the top executives can understand the entire system and direct it successfully from that position. But as organizations evolve, they become more networked and diverse and can only be understood from many perspectives. The earlier assumption that you can view and direct from one viewing point doesn't hold for complex networked organizations.

The ability to run on local expertise starts with embracing the assumption that knowledge and expertise is widely dispersed throughout an organization. Shifting from the assumption that *knowledge and expertise rests at the top* of the organization to **knowledge resides throughout the organization** changes our leadership focus and behavior. In this new reality, we need to look beyond ourselves to the rest of the organization and assess who has the knowledge and expertise that will be helpful for the problem that is presenting itself. Then we need to actively seek out that expertise by including this person and their knowledge in the decision-making process. This practice goes against the traditional rule of positional leadership—that the leader should know everything. The new rule is that leaders need to know what they do not know and acknowledge that there are others who know more than they do in their organization.

We need to let go of barriers to communication and feedback flow. In a rapidly changing world, the lack of feedback diminishes the evolution of our thinking and can lead an organization to stagnate. Yet, organizational communications research has found that information is censored as it goes up a hierarchical organization. Often positional leaders do not receive honest feedback and thus they do not have all the information or knowledge that exists in the organization. Without having feedback that fully informs their decisions, the CEO may make decisions that are not in the organization's best interest. Worse yet, they may not receive any feedback about the fallout from their decisions, reinforcing their perception (and arrogance) that they made the right decision. If employees are censoring or not telling the truth about a CEOs ideas or perspectives, it can lead to a rigidity of thought that eventually causes a collapse of their business.

3. We need to recognize and embrace the uniqueness of local environments.

Nature depends on local expertise because living systems need to be uniquely designed to fit the particular conditions of their environment. Organizations are living systems, and thus they are complex, interdependent, and dynamic and like nature, need to be designed for uniqueness, not uniformity. Universal solutions don't fit the diversity and variation found within organizations. We need to recognize the uniqueness of local environments (teams, departments, divisions etc.) and embrace local expertise to design solutions that allow for customization.

This shift sets up a new relationship between the top of an organization and its local environments, leading us to see local knowledge as an essential asset that is needed to design good solutions appropriate for the particular location. It introduces a co-creation mindset that recognizes that knowledge is spread throughout the system.

> *In addition to feasibility, effectiveness, and achievement,*
> *we add this criterion: Does this solution fit with our organization,*
> *sector, culture, department, and locale?*

As mentioned earlier, 3M and Google have acknowledged that their employees can see possibilities based on where they sit in the organization and their skills and interests. They recognize that the best solutions are found in the co-creation between local expertise and the larger system. Their goal is to unleash these employees to drive their innovative culture.

When we adopt nature's design principle of depending on local expertise, another measure of quality in decision-making emerges. Depending on local expertise enables us to access local input and creates a stronger understanding of critical elements that need to be considered in decision-making.

We need to let go of the assumption that there are universal solutions. While we may have let go of some of our conscious use of machines as models for our organizations and how we treat our employees, there are still many ways that this mindset still affects our decisions and policies. For instance, this thinking shows up in how we list the specifications one must meet for contract bids, requests for proposals, even job descriptions and recruitment. Rather than speaking in nuanced terms of what the contracts or jobs entail and what qualities and talents would be the best fit, we tend to list the same universal qualifications required for every job and ask applicants to respond in kind.

This is particularly true in management where concepts such as management by objectives, Six Sigma, total quality management etc. were universally applied across organizations regardless of context or culture. The assumption being if it worked well in one organization, it would work well in others. This notion has become deeply embedded in our practices. But while using mass-production techniques may be useful for making cars; it is not a good practice for living organizations. Ideas can be scaled across from one human context to another, but they need to be adapted to the uniqueness of the people and culture of the organization. Leadership in a living system requires us to let go of the assumption that there are universal solutions that fit all contexts.

4. We need to recognize emergent practice based in local expertise.

The traditional approach to evaluating programs in an organization is to assess if the programs reflect the best thinking in the field. In nonprofits, this is called evidence-based practice. Acquiring federal and state funding often depends on an organization's ability to demonstrate that they have designed their programs following the best data and evidence. The deep background assumption behind evidence-based practice is that the data and knowledge is universal and should be applied without regard to the local context. This assumption leads us to a "one size fits all" mentality and influences the way we make decisions and develop strategy. But in reality, best practices have a very limited application in complex dynamic systems.

We need to let go of the belief that best practice is a good fit for our level of organizational complexity. The design principle that nature depends on local expertise comes from the appreciation that each context and system is unique and complex. If we grasped the complexity of our organizations, we would let go of the concept of best practice recognizing that it cannot possibly capture the uniqueness of each local context. This change of perception would lead us to shift from evidence-based practice (universally applied) to practice-based evidence. This shift acknowledges that to do good, effective and meaningful work, we need to depend on local expertise and its insights into how local practice informs and shapes work. We would then train all of our front-line workers to scan their environment and recognize patterns. We would regularly harvest their perceptions and thoughts to inform ongoing adaptive cycles for our organization, much like nature's species do in an ongoing instinctual way.

5. We need to recognize the waste involved in not recognizing and utilizing local expertise.

Soil has genetic memory. It knows what grows best on a specific slope with a particular amount of water and sunlight (Benyus, 2002). When we try to grow things that don't fit these conditions, when we work against the preexisting conditions of the soil, water, sunlight, and location, it requires more energy and is often not as successful. If fertilizer is used, it wipes out the genetic memory in the soil and then the soil requires continual use of the fertilizer to grow the plants it once grew naturally (Benyus, 2002). As positional leaders, we need to learn and seek out what fits with the environment instead of forcing the perceived "universal" solution.

Often when organizations implement a universal solution, there is a cost in both the oversight and implementation of the solution. Since the directive comes from outside the local context, it often takes additional staff time to ensure the solution is being applied locally. And if the "universal" solution does not fit with the local context, the local staff struggles to implement it. This costs the organization productivity and increases the frustration of staff who, familiar with the local conditions, often know a better and often simpler and less costly way to solve the problem. These directives have additional repercussions as they affect the relationship between the local staff and the larger organization. Local staff may actively resist implementing the new approach or they may choose to remain quiet about how it could be done with less energy and cost. If this ever comes to light, the staff's withholding can reinforce the assumption that the staff requires oversight, a costly reinforcing cycle.

Paradoxically, when organizations block employees from sharing their expertise, the staff can become dependent on the direction of the positional leaders. The long-term costs of this are that the employee's local expertise is shut down and not available to the organization in the future. It can also overburden managers with the responsibilities for leading a team that doesn't actively cooperate to achieve the organization's mission. Any savings that could have been made by incorporating adaptive applications are lost to the organization.

We need to let go of compensation models that assume there is no local expertise. Traditional compensation assumptions are built on and reinforce the belief that the people at the top of the organization hold the knowledge and strategic capacity to direct the organization. However, as we have discussed, leaders need local expertise. They also need others to implement and accomplish organizational successes. If we appreciate local expertise as a key resource for decisions and solutions, we need to reexamine how we compensate people in organizations. Depending on local expertise challenges the idea that the credit for organizational success lies only at the top of the organization and that CEOs should be primarily compensated for the success. When organizational efficiency, effectiveness, and productivity are helped by creating a distributive leadership structure, traditional compensation models need to change to reflect the value that the staff brings to the organization.

The summary below shows how our focus would shift, what assumptions we would let go of, if we used nature's principle to "depend on local expertise and self-organization" and applied it to our organizations.

1. We need to create and support self-organizing employee cultures.
   - *We need to let go of the assumption that the only source of intelligence rests at the top.*

2. We need to recognize and seek out knowledge, experience, and expertise wherever it exists.
   - *We need to let go of barriers to communication and feedback flow.*

3. We need to recognize and embrace the uniqueness of local environments.
   - *We need to let go of the assumption that there are universal solutions.*

4. We need to recognize emergent practice based in local expertise.
   - *We need to let go of the belief that best practice is a good fit for our level of organizational complexity.*

5. We need to recognize the waste involved in not recognizing and utilizing local expertise.
   - *We need to reexamine compensation models that assume there is no local expertise.*

Questions to Consider:

Traditional leadership has been built on assumptions of hierarchical organizations that: a) expertise rests at the top of the organization; b) change is initiated only at the top; and c) that all responsibility, risks, and rewards rest at the top of the organization. As our organizations become more networked and complex, these traditional assumptions are more and more out of place and create dysfunction in the relationships between employees and management.

To become a generous organization, we need to let go of old assumptions and embrace new ones that match the dynamics found in nature. Nature can be a good teacher to examine how it optimizes self-organization to accomplish things with a light or no supervisory footprint.

Here are some questions that can help us start this journey. I would suggest that one or more of these questions could be used over the course of a year at leadership team meetings. A question could be handed out before the meeting and each person would be asked to reflect on the question. During the meeting, they could share their thoughts with each other. The goal could be to develop strategies, or it could be to generate more powerful questions to ponder for the next meetings. Sometimes powerful questions are effective in creating change because they draw our attention and naturally shift our behavior.

- *Why don't top-down leaders understand the limits of their knowledge and experience?*
- *Why do we assume that local action requires top-down direction and oversight?*
- *How can we shift our understanding, so we can see the intelligence and expertise located nearest the source?*
- *What do our employees believe? Do they expect to be directed by positional leaders? And if so, how can we act so that they see that there are other ways that they can participate and contribute?*
- *What teams in our organization model self-organization? What can we learn from them?*
- *What processes and structures would encourage self-organization in our workplaces?*

- *How can we create distributive leadership throughout our organization?*
- *How can we design policies and leadership practices so that local expertise is unleashed and utilized?*
- *What would our organizations or governmental policies look like if we assumed that knowledge, experience, and expertise existed at the local level in our organizations or communities?*

CHAPTER NINE

Nature Taps the Power of Limits

I like to garden. One thing I have learned from this hobby is that life thrives in my garden if I work within the limits of the environment in which I live. When I take into consideration the temperature, moisture and soil conditions, I can create a beautiful garden that continues to bloom and grow year after year. However, if I want to grow something that's not meant for my climate zone, I need to invest extra effort and time to help that plant continue to bloom. For example, I love dahlias, but they can't survive our winter temperatures, so I must dig them up at the end of the summer and replant them in the spring. The rhododendrons I loved as a child growing up in Pennsylvania don't grow in Minnesota, so I settle for a hybrid variety that is designed to withstand colder temperatures. And while I will never see palm trees out my window, I am fortunate to see majestic oaks, maples, pine and spruce trees at home in my world.

Nature doesn't have the same types of plant and animal life all over the earth. Nature acknowledges the power of limits and works within them to create diverse ecosystems that are filled with plant and animal life that can thrive in that particular setting. By tapping into these limits, nature creates remarkable creatures perfectly adapted to what can seem like the most inhospitable locations. The species of each location evolves to fit with the terrain and other local conditions. They adapt their shapes, needs and abilities to fit the climate whether it is the heat and humidity of the tropics, the dry heat of the desert, or the cold and snowy mountain terrain. They are often so finely adapted to their locale that they cannot survive anywhere else. Take the life forms that inhabit the Antarctica, such as the King Penguins, Weddell seals or the Antarctic Skua. They all thrive in these cold climates, but would die if they were dropped in the Nebraska Sand Hills, just as the prairie dogs, mule deer, and the 720 native grasses and sand tolerant plants would die in the Antarctica.

As humans, we can also tap into the power of limits and use them to creatively adapt to our location and circumstances. When we proactively respond to limits in money, or time, we are using these limits to motivate us to innovate. A book titled *A Beautiful Constraint: How to Transform Your Limitations into Advantages and Why It's Everyone's Business* is filled with wonderful examples, processes and framing on how we can use limits to force innovation (Morgan & Barden, 2015). For example, the founder of IKEA, Ingvar Kamprad proactively imposed a constraint when he started his furniture business. He thought it was easy to make well-designed expensive furniture. He imposed the challenge of making well-designed sustainable furniture that was reasonably priced. In doing so, he was able to create products, indeed an entire store that catered to this market. As this demonstrates, limits are not just about negatively imposing constraints on what we can do. There can be a "positive" power to limits as well. There is a generative power of limits that encourages us to foster something new, more fitting and appropriate to the situation, and usually better than what we had imagined.

When we acknowledge limits, it opens up opportunities for innovation. There are many instances of this. When a group of architects faced the fact that our traditional energy supplies are limited, they identified readily available resources and began experimenting with earth homes[7] and passive solar energy by building homes with south facing exposure. Through these innovations, they were tapping the power of limits. Just as others did when they started using geothermal energy to provide sustainable energy in residential homes, using the constant temperature of the earth to heat and cool our homes. In 2003, a municipal worker in Ellensburg, Washington pulled together grant money and community funds to build the first solar community garden. It enabled individuals who couldn't put solar arrays (series of solar panels) on their homes because of tree cover, to buy solar panels in a community array to reduce their carbon footprint. There now are dozens of such community energy facilities and groups operating and planned around North America.[8] By accepting limits and then using them to fuel creative ideas and solutions, we drive innovation in our lives and our organizations.

I have spent many years working in organizations building annual budgets. The budget process is a wonderful illustration of the variety of human responses to limits embedded in organizations. Sometimes we use limits as a rationale to protect the assets of our department or division, sometimes we use them to justify self-interest or encourage collaboration, and sometimes we use limits to innovate and see how we can leverage what we have to serve the higher purpose of the organization. When we choose the latter option, we see how the power of limits can be tapped to assess our staffing patterns and our traditional assumptions of resource allocation in new and creative ways.

We can also take lessons from nature's principle of "form follows function" (Chapter Four) and see if our *forms* are still serving the core *function* of the organization. When I have experienced this kind of thoughtful and creative budgeting in organizations, I have seen how it can bring people together to be innovative about how to thrive within the limits of the organization.

---

[7] Earth homes utilize surrounding terrain or other natural elements such as dirt, bamboo, wood, and clay to create a space with a negligible environmental impact. http://inhabitat.com/8-inexpensive-earth-homes-almost-anyone-can- afford/.

[8] http://blog.solargardens.org/2010/08/brief-history-of-solar-gardens.html

How does nature's lesson of "tapping the power of limits" help us to think differently about leadership?

I am a biker and I own several fancy bikes. They have 30 gears and are designed to go fast. When I was visiting Amsterdam a few years ago, I took a couple of bike tours out of the city. Most of the rental bikes were simple three-speed bikes with high handle bars to make it comfortable to sit upright while biking. I didn't see many bikes that were like the ones I owned. I wondered what led the owners to choose this kind of bike. Then I noticed that people in Amsterdam use bikes for daily transportation to and from work, to get groceries, and do errands. The Netherlands is relatively flat, so other than wind or weather, there aren't many challenges to overcome. It struck me that the bikes in Amsterdam used only the engineering that they needed. It made me wonder about the appeal of *over-engineering* things. What is the attraction of having all the bells and whistles even if we don't use them?

We see this dynamic in the technology software and hardware we buy, the cars we drive, and the bikes we own, just to name a few instances. Is there something intrinsic to the American culture that feeds the desire to use more energy and resources than we need to accomplish something? Can we learn something important from nature that could help us rethink the amount of energy we use?

1. We need to use only the amount of energy a problem needs.

What is the smallest amount of resources or energy we can use to gain the biggest impact? This is the question that I have been asking since I became familiar with the "power of limits" design principle from biomimicry. Living systems are connected and dynamic. If we understand the variables, relationships, and links in a living system, we can see the small leverage points that if we nudge here, pull there, or add in a design principle the rest of the system will help bring everything into a resilient balance.

In my consulting practice, I have applied this principle to strategic planning, culture change, leadership, decision-making, and problem solving. For instance, by keeping this idea in mind, I start from the premise that just because we have time, doesn't mean we need to waste it in planning meetings or getting more people involved than we need to for making decisions. The challenge is to fit the right amount of energy with the task we want to accomplish, using a constraint to encourage creative approaches to planning or strengthening our organizational culture.

We need to let go of the assumption that emotions don't have place in our organizations. In fact, emotions can play a significant role in the organizational dynamics that surround limits. When people are afraid, don't trust each other, or feel the need to control everything, we tend to design processes that use more energy than is really needed to get things done. This design principle, helps me pause and ask, is it possible to do this in less time or with less effort and still get excellent results? If so, can we imagine how we could approach the work differently to make it more effective and efficient? In the next chapter, I will share some examples of this dynamic at work in organizational culture change and strategic planning.

We need to let go of our tendency to deny the limits that exist in our organizations. When we deny the power of limits and what they reveal about our situation, we end up expending extra energy to overcome them. Holding unrealistic assumptions about what people are expected to give to an organization or misplaced attachments to outdated programs or products can be costly. For example, we don't always recognize the limits of our employees' time, energy, or willingness to sacrifice. We ask them to give more and more time to complete a project without understanding its impact on their personal or family lives. This can add to the dysfunction in the workplace as employees become disgruntled or burnt out. And sometimes we continue programs that we should discontinue because we deny the feedback that they are no longer relevant to our customers or clients. Keeping a product line or program after it has run its course reinforces protective self-interested behavior and delegitimizes feedback from the external environment. These behaviors can create a subculture in an organization that works against the development of a generous organization.

On the other hand, we may recognize the extra effort and decide that it is still worth pursuing. For example, in gardening if I want to plant roses in my colder climate, I need to create a buffer against the cold to help them make it through the winter. This can include digging a trench, laying them into it, covering the trench over with dirt and then layering the top with bales of hay.

This trenching technique will help protect them from winter temperatures. Each of these tasks takes time and energy. As a gardener, I must decide if ignoring the limits of my gardening zone is worth the extra time and effort.

2. We need to align with the purpose and direction of our living organization.

Traditional leadership sees organizations as inert or machine-like. From this perspective, organizations do not have their own purpose. Instead they are seen as tools for positional leaders to use to achieve their own ends, often to make more money for those at the top. Living systems, on the other hand, have a higher shared purpose. Leaders of living systems co-create the purpose with their organization, by asking, "What deep need has the organization been created to serve?" The question has to do with what the organization wants to serve, produce, and how it creates conditions for life of future generations. Sometimes this purpose is found in the organization's culture which gives voice to its meaning and to the direction it wants to go. The culture is the combination of beliefs, values, and unconscious assumptions which shape individual and collective behavior in an organization. Looking closely at the culture can help us see the living system and its purpose.

> *If we can align the direction of our leadership with our organizational purpose, the system will help us achieve these mutual goals, if we let it.*

What does it mean that the "system will help us achieve" the purpose of the organization? Let's take a look. We've all probably known a newly hired positional leader who did not recognize or support the programs of their predecessor or the culture of the organization. In such a case, a new CEO wanted to remake a foundation to fit with his own agenda and interests. The foundation had a history of signature programs that had demonstrated excellent value and impact over decades of work in their region. But the new CEO dismantled these important programs and replaced them with initiatives he wanted. This led to an exodus of talented staff and leadership. It was the board's job to sort out the competing perspectives and feedback the organization and the CEO were giving them. While the board didn't think of the foundation as a living system, they did pay attention to its history, contribution, and culture and saw the misalignment. The board had to discern if the CEO was the right fit with the foundation, they asked, "Did the foundation want to remain as it was, or was it going through an adaptive cycle to prepare for the next phase of its work?" After considering this question, they realized that CEO's leadership was not helping the foundation achieve its highest purpose. The CEO was fired from his job because his ego had superseded the foundation's purpose.

If we reread this question "Did the foundation want to remain as it was, or was it going through an adaptive cycle to prepare for the next phase of its work?" as if we were talking about an individual's desire and purpose, it wouldn't seem strange. However, because we aren't used to seeing an organization as a living system, this paragraph may be disorienting. Nevertheless, I have found if you go in the direction that the living organization wants, everything is easier. Change is faster and more sustainable if we use the dynamics of a living system to design organizational interventions. It is as if the organization is helping the work to move forward more rapidly.

We need to let go of fear-based behavior that drives a scarcity mentality. There is a difference between seeing limits and having a scarcity mentality. Limitations often are signals from the external environment that an adaptive action is required for an organization's business model to either remain as is or evolve to succeed. Tapping the power of limits requires us to see constraints as positive (Morgan & Barden, 2015). But instead of seeing constraints as fuel for innovation and adaptation, we tend to see limitations as something to fear. When the emotion of fear occupies our mind, our thinking shifts to scarcity instead of abundance and begins to impact all our actions. In an organization, a scarcity mentality causes us to cooperate less, protect more, develop a victim mentality, and behave in ways that diminish our relationships with each other. It can be a source of tension for employees and a rationale to treat other employees and clients poorly.

Leaders of generous organizations notice the scarcity mentality and its accompanying emotion of fear and recognize the danger it signals for the culture of the organization. Fear diminishes trust between people and causes the organization to hunker down—the opposite stance of an innovative generous organization. Instead, we need to use the limitation as a way to get people thinking about what needs to change for the organization to become more adaptive and thrive.

3. We need to develop and strengthen distributive leadership

Nature's living system works because all the species and plant life are in a relationship with each other. Each individual species' self-interests are served when the larger ecology thrives, thus all their efforts have this as their ultimate focus. The organizational parallel to this dynamic is the creation of leader-full organizations. If leadership is distributed throughout the organization (distributive leadership), it means employees are actively engaged in taking initiative in service of the organization's highest purpose.

There are three reasons why distributive leadership is important in a living organization. First, distributive leadership provides leadership and initiative at all levels of the organization that can be used to serve the larger organization. It provides feedback about changes in the internal and external environments and what adaptations are needed so that the organization can thrive. Second, it provides bench strength, continually developing the next generation of leadership and management, increasing its likelihood to be successful and long lasting. And third, it recognizes and supports more individual capacity and individual initiative (self-organizing) at all levels which increases the organization's adaptive capacity, flexibility, and agility.

One way to develop distributive leadership in an organization is to design a system that intentionally hires, rewards, and provides feedback on the five essential characteristics that individual employees need to display in the workplace.

1. Ability to initiate and organize their own work and learning. For leadership to exist throughout an organization, employees must be able to initiate and organize their own work. This means they have an internal locus of control, so they don't have to wait to be told or ask their supervisor what they should do. They also need to initiate their own learning in the workplace.

2. Ability to accurately assess their strengths and weaknesses. To focus learning, employees who engage in distributive leadership must have an accurate assessment of their strengths and weaknesses. They must be able to ascertain what they need to know, or perhaps better put, what they do not know. If they are oblivious, out of touch, or too arrogant to see their strengths and weaknesses, they will not focus on what they need to learn. Self-deception significantly encumbers the development of distributive leadership.

3. Ability to align to the highest shared purpose of the organization. Employees must understand how their day-to-day work aligns and contributes to the purpose of the organization. But we often don't do a very good job at helping employees see the meaning in their work. Remember the story about the three brick layers? The first one was just laying brick, the second was building a wall, and the third was contributing to building a cathedral. For distributive leadership to work, employees need to see how they are contributing to the larger purpose, how they are building a cathedral. If this alignment doesn't happen, we get something very different. I call it empowerment gone wild.

4. Ability to be aware of and manage their emotions. An individual employee may have all the above capacities, but if they are unaware of or can't manage their own emotions at work, they can wreak havoc in a team and with their colleagues. Therefore, distributive leadership requires that individual employees be emotionally intelligent. The more employees who can read group dynamics, have empathy for others, as well as recognize and manage their own emotions, the stronger the collective emotional intelligence of the organization will be.

5. Ability to have active hope. People can have passive hope where they look for someone else to fix the problem for them, or be hopeless where they give up and just try to survive. Active hope is about behaving every day in a way to

bring the desired future into being (Macy & Johnstone, 2012). This active hope mindset is necessary for innovative thought. It enables individuals to show up and create the world that they want to see, even if at first glance they don't seem to have the influence or position to make that possible. In living systems, innovation bubbles up from the bottom, so having people with distributive leadership capacities and an active hope in what's possible and in what they can do, leads to an organizational culture of innovation (Jennings & Dooley, 2007).

We need to learn to let go of top-down leadership with an emphasis on control. Organizations will always have positional leaders, people in authority who have the responsibility to ensure the organization's strategic direction and purpose is clear. But we need to let go of the belief that top-down management needs to control others below them. After years of experience, I have come to see that good leaders and managers are more about facilitating and developing and coaching their staff members (Smart, 2005).

The summary below shows how our focus would shift, what assumptions we would let go of, if we used nature's principle to "tap the power of limits" and applied it to our organizations.

1. **We need to use only the amount of energy a problem needs.**
   - *We need to let go of the assumption that emotions don't have a place in our organizations.*
   - *We need to let go of our tendency to deny the limits that exist in our organizations.*

2. **We need to align with the purpose and direction of our living organization.**
   - *We need to let go of fear-based behavior that drives a scarcity mentality.*

3. **We need to develop and strengthen distributive leadership.**
   - *We need to let go of top-down leadership with an emphasis on control.*

Questions to Consider:

I have concluded that here in the U.S., we have a difficulty taping the power of limits. Instead, we tend to see limits as a challenge to work around. In nature, limits allow species to adapt and thrive ensuring the long-term sustainability and resilience of the system. Constraints create a hot bed of innovation and can help us adapt to changes in the external environment. How can we embrace limits and see the constraints they impose as beautiful?

Often constraints and limits trigger an emotional response. We see the limit of funding as a trigger for fear that there won't be enough. Fear and scarcity are often accompanied by feeling like a victim of circumstance. Fear, scarcity, and victimization are emotions that undermine generous organizations. We need to shift from seeing limits in terms of scarcity and instead tap into how they can aid innovation. Here are some questions that can help our organizations see limits and how we are responding to them.

- *How can we learn to accept limits that exist in our organization?*
- *What is the intrinsic value of recognizing limits in our organizations?*
- *How can we make a constraint beautiful?*
- *How well do we help people move their emotions from fear to possibility and hope? How can we do this better?*
- *What constraints do we want to proactively impose on our organization to drive the next round of innovation?*
- *What are ways of enhancing resources through partnerships rather than internally thinking we must raise more funds for ourselves alone?*
- *Where is leadership in our organization? What can we do to make distributive leadership work in our organization?*

CHAPTER TEN

Leading from a Living Systems Mindset

When I first started to work in organizations I was told that change starts at the top, but quickly realized that that type of change rarely disappears into the day-to-day life of the organization. Rather, it tends to stand out as something brought in from above and overlaid on top of the existing structures and processes. To be successful at incorporating this style of change takes a great deal of time, resources, and supervision.

Strategic planning is a typical example of how organizations create change. Leadership and management rarely engage the affected employees in these plans. They spend many hours thoughtfully developing a plan, then roll it out to employees, align work plans and annual goals to support the plan, and then supervise the hell out of it. Strategic plans are linear. They start in a specific year and move forward with specific delineated steps. The goals and objectives of the plan are initiated and reported on over on key dates within the plan. While there can be some adaptation, it rarely deviates from the original strategic goals.

Nature doesn't do change this way. Nature is a living system and its strategies can only be understood from this viewpoint. Nature doesn't do linear plans. Nature works in adaptive cycles and the flow and content of the cycle is firmly connected to the external environment. It is always engaged in an observing, learning, acting cycle, so that it can know what changes are taking place and how it needs to adapt. By learning to adapt to what is going on in the wider environment or ecosystem it enhances its resiliency. Because the external environment is in constant change, the adaptive cycle is also dynamic.

Since adaptive cycles are continuous, nature doesn't need a discrete strategic plan to thrive. But it does require all entities in the ecosystem to be actively engaged in their individual observing, learning, acting cycles. From this feedback, change initially happens at the local level, in a way that constantly evolves the species and its relationship to the environment. This then pushes adaptive capacity throughout the system. In this dynamic environment, relationships form, sustain, shift, and die. The larger environment then takes this shift into account to continually create conditions conducive to future generations of life. That is its primary objective.

> *When our leadership is informed by and paces the dynamics of living systems, our interventions and solutions disappear into the system.*

If we see organizations as living systems, these lessons from nature help us see how to lead differently. Instead of layering change onto the surface of the organization, as in traditional strategic plans, nature shows us how to design change so that it disappears into the organization's day-to-day life. For example, in my consulting practice I worked with an organization that wanted to experiment with new ways to create and think about strategic plans.

The challenge: Traditional strategic plans identify goals and strategies in three-year timelines. But in today's rapidly changing environment, it is difficult for a traditional plan to remain relevant for three years. The challenge was to provide a strategic direction for the organization in a highly turbulent external environment. The strategic framework we developed was an experiment in meeting this challenge.

The goals of the design of the strategic plan were threefold:

- *To build scanning capacity in the staff and board to help the organization pay attention to the external environment and how it needs to adapt to changes and challenges that are triggered by it.*
- *To build strategic thinking capacity within the staff at all levels.*
- *To create a three-year strategic focus for the organization that provides direction and flexibility to respond to the changing landscape within the non-profit sector*

The Process: We also experimented with building organizational capacity for ongoing scanning of the external environment in the staff. We generated a team composed of staff and board members to scan the internal organization and external environment. Nine staff and three board members met and were provided with frameworks for scanning. They identified 46 topics/areas to scan and these were divided up between staff and board members according to their interest and ability to gather data. The topics ranged from funding trends, demographics, market forces, organizational culture and leadership, partnerships programs and services, social media, technology, facilities, earned income opportunities, and trends in the sector. Individuals gathered information from reports (state, federal, sector), data analysis, conversations with thought leaders in the field, interviews with partners (current and possible), site visits (facilities), and observation. Each scanner created an executive summary of their findings by topic. They held two meetings to share, analyze, and make meaning of what was collected.

We included an annual generation of goals and objectives that related to the powerful strategic questions. These goals were adapted to what was going on in the external environment and were based on the organization's ongoing observations and learning.

Well-packed questions: Instead of locking the organization into a specific set of initiatives, we framed the strategy by asking powerful questions. A "well-packed question" is one that doesn't have an easy answer. These types of questions attract attention and energy to them over time. It allows a person or organization to continually be aware of the strategic direction, while responding to the day-to-day adaptive challenges it faces. We identified four powerful questions:

1. Who are we becoming?
2. How can we optimize and expand our relationships (with stakeholders and through partnerships)?
3. How might our programs need to change and adapt in the future?
4. What organizational structure, culture, and leadership philosophy would help us be adaptive and innovative?

The first question related to a mission imperative. In a traditional strategic plan, this question is likely to be "Who are we?" and through the question, the organization revisits the vision, mission, and values of the organization and once done, puts the revisions in place. The goal is then accomplished.

The question "Who are we (the organization) becoming?" draws attention to how the organization is evolving and responding to changing external conditions. It assumes that the organization is not stagnant but that it will take on many forms and structures as it achieves its core purpose and it will continually adapt to respond to opportunities that will help it thrive into the future. In this way, it is like a mountain stream that as it travels to sea level will continually change its form to adapt to the changing landscapes it flows through along the way. In its journey, there will be waterfalls, rapids, backwaters, eddies, slow wide rivers and deep running rapids.

We used these questions to provide a strategic direction while allowing the goals and objectives to change annually to adapt to opportunities and threats that appear on the non-profit landscape.

The goals organize around the questions, but also reflect what the organization and its leadership are seeing in their environment. For example, it is obvious that over the next three years, the organization will be approached about additional mergers or will consider acquisitions. The question "who are we becoming?" allows for goals and objectives that reflect that reality and the challenges that go with it.

We found this process had a powerful impact on how the staff engaged with and supported the strategic planning process. Because they gained insight into the external environment through their involvement with the scanning, they not only paid attention to the strategy but actively supported it. At the end of the first year, an assessment of progress on strategic initiatives reaped a large number of adaptations and actions that supported the strategic plan. Many more than would typically be identified. The organization and the staff all benefitted from this process, leading to a high level of commitment to the strategic plan and a more generous successful system.

Another example of how a strategic plan can work with the dynamics of a living system occurred in my work with a public/private association. The organization wanted to intentionally learn from nature and apply its design principles to the organization. Accordingly, while it wanted a strategic plan, it was open to something non-traditional. Our work started with a one-page articulation of the organization and its primary directive, entitled *A Culture of Impact*. This document conveyed what they care about, what they do, and what impact they seek to make. It turned out to be a powerful graphic that made the larger purpose of the organization visible to funders, members, employees, and external stakeholders.

The document was paired with the organization's *Adaptive Cycle* which drew on the ecocycle that we explored in Chapter Four as an aid for their planning discussions. Using the ecocycle, they identified what they intended to explore, launch, sustain, and release over the next three years. We assumed that the items would continue to evolve and be released as the external conditions changed. Each month the management committee reviewed the adaptive cycle and changed it as needed. Using this adaptive cycle, members of the committee are now much more attuned to changes in the external environment and are able to shift their thinking based on the opportunities and challenges that emerged. They see how the organization needs to fit within the larger environment and understand that when they are attuned to this external dynamic, they can more effectively achieve the impact they are seeking.

How does leading from a living systems mindset help us to think about leadership differently?

As leaders, we need to focus on the dynamics of living systems. When we combine our understanding of how living systems behave and design our leadership with these dynamics in mind, we lead more effectively and with more sustainable impact. In Chapter One, we identified the seven key dynamics that exist in living systems. When leaders understand and lead in a way that complements these dynamics, everything we do is easier and more sustainable. In the following sections, I will revisit these dynamics and share how I have incorporated this living system framework in my work and how it has enabled organizations to become more self-sustaining, resilient and generous.

1.Living systems are interdependent—change in one part of the system influences other parts of the system in expected and unexpected ways.

Living systems are interdependent; change in one part of the system influences other parts in expected and unexpected ways. How can we learn to be aware of the connections within our organizations, and between our organizations and the outside world? One way is to assume interdependence and see how it makes us more conscious of our mindsets and how things work within the organization. For example, do we assume that something we share with a colleague on email will stay with just that person? Or do we recognize relationships, ties, and connections between people, so we can reasonably assume that what we share with one person will be shared all along those lines of relationships? Do we see ourselves as part of both the problems and solutions in our organizations? Or do we see ourselves as standing apart from those organizational issues or problems? Here are some lessons that I have learned in consulting when I assume interdependence.

As you'll recall, we have used two primary metaphors to think about organizations. The first one is that organizations operate like a machine. Machines are filled with parts that are linked in an intentional way, but generally behave as if they are separate from each other. Machines need an outside power source to turn on and run. Machines behave rationally and predictability. You can control a machine through orders and directions and how they are engineered.

Living systems are dynamic and evolving. They are networked and connected. When humans are involved, they are also emotional. Living systems are filled with relationships and ties. The more you understand the variables, patterns, and connections, the more you understand the leverage points that can be used to influence the system (Meadows, 2008).

Because machines need power to operate, we tend to gather more power than we need to manage the organization and to create change. This strategy works well for a machine, but it works against us in a living system. Try substituting these default behaviors with the following questions and approaches:

> *What is the lightest touch we can make to generate the highest impact?*
> *What is the smallest thing you can do to generate the highest impact?*

These seemingly simple questions have opened up a world of possibilities, that I call gentle and high impact action.

Gentle action: Because our organizations are living systems and all living systems are interconnected, we cannot separate ourselves from our organizations. We can behave as if we are separate, but this just isn't the case, our behaviors will cause consequences, both big and small, within the organization. Therefore, instead of driving decisions down from the top, we should begin to see ourselves as part of the system and part of what needs to be changed (Peat, 2008). When we assume that our actions will continue to ripple through the relationship ties, it leads us to using gentle action, to having a lighter touch in leading our organizations.

High impact: Because all things are connected, small tweaks can generate significant impact. For example, powerful questions can act like an attractor in an organization. A well-worded, well-packed question can provoke a thoughtful response because it doesn't have an obvious answer. It leads people to think about their answer more deeply, and this act of inquiry can shift behaviors.

For example, I used to work at a women's college. We did a series of focus groups with our students to develop a deeper understanding of their college experience from their point of view. Their answers showed that they felt very supported developmentally. However, they couldn't name ways that they had been equally challenged. Based on this information, I posed the following questions to my staff: Are we challenging our students to become the best they can be? And if so, in what ways, and if not, what do we need to change? Within three weeks, they shared at staff meetings how they had shifted their behavior to increase the level of challenge they gave to their students. I didn't put the goal of increasing challenge in a strategic plan or a work plan. All I did was ask the question. It was enough to get the staff members to notice what they were and weren't doing. It was a small act that generated high impact.

Beneficial virus: I have also seen how a "beneficial virus" can be spread throughout an organization. Organizations run on meaning. What we talk about matters. When one sees connections, influencing change can occur along lines of relationships (Allen & Cherry 2000). We can intentionally spread ideas through conversations and relationships that help people understand and pass on powerful ideas. When we talk about things that matter, people will repeat the conversation through their network. Social media is a perfect example of this; in fact we often speak of a tweet or YouTube video going viral.

We also need to recognize that in an interdependent living system change can come from anywhere. When people share their insights, observations, suggestions, and solutions through their network, the momentum can push an organization off its equilibrium status and cause it to reach a tipping point that shifts the organization (Peat, 2008).

When we think in terms of connections, we recognize the need to look at the larger picture and the possible ramifications of our decisions. We see the need to develop a strategy to communicate to those who remain why this person was let go. If we don't, people will make up their own reasons which might not serve the organization. We also might need to help the team and other employees figure out how to share the work of that employee until their replacement is found, and perhaps even have the other employees help create a job description that better fits the needs of the organization and the performance expectations.

2. Living systems become more diverse as they evolve.

Living systems evolve. But they do not always evolve in the same way. Nature only achieves a Type III ecology through diversity. It is the mutual relationships between distinct species and plant life that creates a Type III ecology or a generous system.

The difference between an organization that is adapting, learning, and thriving into the future and one that may be making money but will eventually find its business model collapsing, is whether they are becoming more diverse. Without diversity, group think and rigidity in products and beliefs make organizations less adaptive to what is changing in the external environment. When we work from a living systems perspective, helping our organization to become more diverse is important to its evolution. Here are some strategies I have used in my consulting practice to encourage diversity:

Provoke the system with different viewpoints: It used to be assumed that facilitators should be neutral. I now believe that if there is group-think behavior in a team or organization, the role of leadership or a facilitator is also to invite and provoke others to challenge the traditional thinking of the organization. This does not mean that you stop creating a safe space for conversation; in fact the sense of safety may be even more important when handling these kinds of issues and questions. We can help maintain this safe space by stating up front that challenges should be worded not as personal attacks but as open and honest questions intent on serving the larger purpose—and that there will be no personal repercussion from the conversation.

The kind of questions we ask as facilitators will also set the tone. We can start with questions that expand thinking, such as: Does anyone see it differently? How else could we look at this? What are the unquestioned assumptions or mindsets behind our suggested solution? Does this fit with who we are now or want to be in the future? What are the possible unintended consequences that may occur if we chose this decision?

Build diversity into the organization to support evolution in the organization: Nature depends on diversity to build resilient ecosystems. The underlying assumption is that to build generous ecologies, we need mutualistic relationships between very different species, where the waste of one becomes a nutrient for another. This exchange of nutrients is what makes ecosystems generous and sustainable.

Organizationally we need diversity to evolve beyond our own thinking and the limits of our individual world views. If we have a board and senior team made up of older white males, they will see the marketplace from their experience. However, the products that they think are needed in the world will likely be different than those needed by the young mom, the Somali immigrant, or someone from the millennial generation. By not having gender and ethnic parity in an organization, we miss vital information, perspective, and insight into different markets and the products that serve them. In nature, a lack of diversity diminishes the resilience of the system. In organizations, the lack of institutional diversity also weakens their future resilience (Taylor & Wacker, 1997).

Opposition is necessary for wholeness: To understand the benefits of a living system, one must be open to perceptions and realities that are different from their own. Nature, a living system, is designed as a network. Organizations are also networked which means there is no single point from which to view and understand the whole. Therefore, to fully appreciate and support the complex, dynamic, networked system, we need to welcome a wide diversity of experience and perspectives of reality. We must welcome opposite points of view to understand the system as a whole (Allen, 2012). When we do this, we not only have greater understanding of the entire system, we will also have the diversity needed to keep our organizations successfully adapting and evolving. Remember, a kite rises against the wind, so don't be afraid of opposition.

Look for non-positional influencers: Another way to invite diversity into decision-making is to look beyond traditional positional managers and leaders. All organizations have non-positional influencers in its social network that can be brought into the decision-making process. For example, the Deluxe Company in Minneapolis studied the social networks within their organization to identify the individuals that influence others but were not positional leaders. They then intentionally brought these individuals into strategic planning sessions to leverage the diversity of their perspectives and incorporate their thinking into decision-making and to help share and disseminate the learnings and programs developed through this process.

3. Living systems are never static, they are always in flux.

What changes when we think that our organizations and the world are in constant movement? First, we wouldn't think that change must be initiated by an outside source to get things going. Instead, we would need to think of how we can transform the energy that already is in movement in the organization.

When we recognize that organizations are in constant movement, we then see organizational strategies as adaptive cycles instead of linear constructs that don't adapt over time. Just like nature, we need to develop an adaptive cycle approach to our organizational work. Our strategic planning needs to be structured and designed to pace the movement of the environment we are in.

Acknowledge and embrace the need to constantly adapt: For example, the adaptive cycle teaches us to let go of our programs and structures so we can invest those resources in the next innovation. Traditional thought, based on an assumption of the wisdom of maintaining the status quo, would encourage organizations to build their market niche and fiercely defend it. But in a dynamic world, that strategy leads to rigidity in thought and in our business model. This fixed position speeds the collapse of a business cycle because the world around us is changing and if we are not, it will pass us by. Kevin Kelly (1998) wrote that technology companies need to learn to let go at the top of their niche and be innovative. If they don't, someone in a garage somewhere will invent the next new thing that will move the mountain out from under them.

Embrace the dynamic movement of living systems. It is not possible to control a dynamic system but we can influence it. Things are in flux. Predictability and control are the next assumptions that fall to the side when there is constant movement and change. Think of a financial advisor looking at the stock market over the course of a day. The stock prices are up and down with their expertise, they can spot patterns but they can't control prices or guarantee specific returns for their investor.

In organizations, most of the problems we have keep morphing as we try to solve them. Additional information and variables show up in predictable and unpredictable ways. Yet, we have leaders who still believe they can control people in their organization. This controlling behavior is just wasted energy. People are very creative at resisting what they don't want to do. It is easier to gain their support by involving them in the process and decision-making, rather than try to control their behavior and force their buy-in.

4. Living systems are filled with feedback loops that facilitate evolution.

Feedback in a living system is how behavior gets reinforced or dampened down. In nature, when a species needs to adapt, the intensity of feedback increases. Feedback starts the cycle, forcing adaptation and facilitating the evolution of the system. Traditionally, organizations restrict feedback if they see themselves as separate from or "above" their environment. For example, they may be open to feedback on their competitive advantage, but less open to feedback on how their behaviors impact the community they are based in or the environment. Feedback from employees to managers can also be dampened down if employees don't trust their supervisor or if the organization discourages and penalizes people who speak their mind. If we see our organizations as living systems, we need to develop a positive relationship to feedback because it is directly connected to our organization's ability to thrive and evolve.

Here are some practices I have used as I shifted my thinking about the importance of feedback.

Strengthen rich and diverse feedback loops: In a machine-like organization, the parts don't need information unless it is directly connected to how the parts are functioning. But living systems need lots of feedback that aren't restricted in scope. Nature recognizes that feedback on relationships, the local ecology and the larger environment are all needed to evolve. Human organizations also need a wide range of information and feedback to learn and evolve. We need feedback to strengthen self-regulation and self-organization – two powerful behaviors in generous organizations.

When I consult with an organization, I intentionally assess the level of feedback that exists in the organization. If there isn't enough feedback, I look for ways to increase the amount and variety of feedback mechanisms employees and others can use. For example, I have helped organizations redesign performance reviews to be based on more than just the feedback from the supervisor. One way is to hear from key colleagues who depend on this employee to help them get their job done. Having them give feedback as well as the supervisor can enrich the feedback to the employee. I have also developed a new process in performance reviews where the employee is expected to seek feedback about themselves from at least three colleagues as source material for the performance review. This supports both their self-organization as well as their learning about themselves.

Sometimes I do 360 reviews for CEOs. For these, I intentionally seek both internal and external feedback. One time, I had a CEO who was struggling with his board and the board was struggling with him. By interviewing external partners and stakeholders, I found that the CEO was very well regarded in the community and the field. This added perspective (feedback) helped the board see the CEO's strengths and it allowed them to work through their other differences.

Notice how your organization restricts feedback: I have also learned that if an organization restricts the feedback and information that the living systems craves, people will create their own version of reality and feedback loops that may be helpful or detrimental to the organization. Knowing this, I also assess what kind of feedback the organization restricts. For example, do the leaders share information they receive by scanning the external environment? Do they keep people looking internally instead of externally? Does communication go downward but not upward? Are there ways to communicate and relate across the organization? Are there organizational backwaters and eddies where feedback is stuck?

What feedback makes a difference? In a networked connected system there is more feedback, but not all feedback is equal. Some feedback is just noise. Once you are attuned to the need, quality and importance of feedback, the next step is to identify what feedback is helpful to the organization's ability to be resilient.

Create feedback that describes and observes without judgment or evaluation: I have also learned that how feedback gets communicated matters. Building capacity in the employees of an organization so that they share information in a non-judgmental or evaluative way helps feedback to be heard and utilized (Caspersen, 2015).

5. Living systems cannot be steered or controlled, only attracted or nudged.

Living systems cannot be controlled. Human beings can be controlled part of the time but not all the time and the controlling entity will expend a lot of energy trying to maintain this control. For parents with teenagers this is an obvious statement. Whereas force creates resistance, living systems (and humans) can be attracted or nudged to move in a direction. When I assume that an organization is a living system, I work and lead differently. This is what I have learned:

Attraction instead of push: When I started my consulting practice, one of the things that intimidated me was marketing my services. I resolved that I would reframe my outreach based on attraction instead of pushing marketing brochures out to potential clients. I also follow these rules within my work; I uniquely design each intervention to fit the distinctive characteristics of the organization. I always provide more value than I charge. And I make sure that real sustainable change has the organization's fingerprints all over the transformation. Because of these simple rules, I haven't had to market my work in the 18 years I have been in business. My clients promote and recommend me to others. New clients are attracted to work with me because they have a recommendation from a colleague they trust.

This applies to organizations as well. People in organizations have sovereignty—the freedom of self-determination. This belief is directly opposed to how we traditionally think about employees. Machine-like organizations believe that employees are paid only to receive directions from managers and CEOs, not to offer anything that is not specifically asked for. This approach precludes the need to attract employees into authentic engagement – and the benefits that accrue from having their input and energy. Instead it supports pushing employees to do what they are being directed to do.

If we want to gain the active support of people, they must be free to choose. I believe in taking the time to attract people to an idea or an issue instead of selling the idea to people. A straightforward way of attracting people to organizational change is to help them see why it matters to them, the organization, and the work.

Let go of strategies that use force, top-down control, and manipulation: I have learned that living systems resist force, top-down control and manipulation. The system may initially comply, but it won't actively support or engage when force or control leads it. And if the force and manipulation continue over time, the leaders will be faced with malicious compliance, which creates significant waste and often makes it impossible to achieve their goals.

Living systems can help accomplish change if you are aligned with its prime directive: Living systems can help us create the change we hope for, if our intentions are aligned with what the larger living system wants. If living systems want to be resilient and thrive, they will help us if that is our intention as well. For example, if a person's own goals are interrelated with the organization in which she works, by accomplishing her goals, the organization will thrive as well. We need to learn to see organizations as active partners and a co-creator in our work, rather than as dead weight.

Nudge and wait: Living systems take time to respond. Traditionally, when we don't get an immediate response, we push harder. In a living organization that is a way to increase resistance. I nudge the system and watch for small signs of movement before I nudge again. For example, I might share an idea or strategy and invite them to reflect on it and bring their thoughts back to the next meeting. This allows time for them to process our conversation and often results in a shift in their thought patterns. If I had pressed them for a response at the time, instead of giving them an invitation to reflect, I would have received resistance. The wait time allows them to adjust to new thoughts, possibilities, or actions. I learned this from walking on wet sand on the beach. Wet sand is hard, and it doesn't leave much of a footprint when walked upon. But if you stand in one place and wait, the wet sand slowly allows our foot to sink into the sand. Wet sand operates like a network. It is made up of grains of sand held together by saline. When it encounters force those elements combine to resist; however, when it encounters a slow entry into its system, it accepts the presence of our foot. Living systems are networked and the nudge and wait for change is very effective in influencing them.

6. Living systems only accept solutions that the system helps to create.

In my experience, people support what they help create. So, the fewer people who are involved in a decision, the fewer people will actively support the decision. In living systems, everyone is engaged. In generous organizations, this expectation of engagement is based on the interdependence embedded in it. Everyone has a unique point of view and when all of those are considered; the final decision is actively supported and disappears into the day-to-day work of the organization. Here are some strategies I have learned for involving people in decision-making:

All important decisions need to have people's fingerprints on them: Some routine decisions don't need involvement, especially if there is a reservoir of trust in the organization. But decisions that matter to people or are important to the organization need to be designed to involve people, so they will support the final decision. Remember that nature depends on local knowledge, in part, because its active involvement helps the system to self-organize and adapt. Tapping local expertise allows them to support the final decision instead of doing work-a-rounds.

Understanding the problem and solution is needed: We need to recognize and name the problem before a solution is generated. People also need to accept that there is a problem, this acceptance is important to gain their support of the solution. Helping people understand the problem is part of the process to engage them in generating a solution. For example, in my work in higher education we had many discussions on increasing our diversity. There were lots of solutions, but those solutions tended to follow from people's perception of the problem. If people thought diversity could be increased by having a more diverse student body, then their solution was found in recruitment. If a person thought diversity could be enhanced by having more diversity in the books that people studied— the solution was curriculum change. We need to agree on the problem first, and then the solution will follow.

Issuing an authentic invitation to engage: Many people who have worked in an organization have stories to tell about being invited to participate in an initiative, decision, or goal. Unfortunately, many of those stories are about inauthentic empowerment. This occurs when a positional leader says he wants to hear what people say about a decision and then ignores what they tell him. This is not only a missed opportunity for valuable feedback and innovative ideas; it leads employees to be dispirited and demoralized. It also means that when next asked, even if the leader means it this time, they are unlikely to offer their best thinking or full support of the eventual outcome.

When we authentically invite people to engage, we get better ideas and solutions. This means that leaders must be open to hearing feedback and be willing to change their minds and direction. That is what an authentic invitation means.

7. Living systems only pay attention to what is meaningful to them here and now.

We need to understand what is meaningful to the living organizations and the people who work there. Why does this issue matter to you? Why does this issue matter to your work? Why does this issue (or strategic goal) matter to the organization? Why does this matter to our world and larger community?

When we show we have heard and are paying attention to their answers to these questions, people will pay attention to what we say. And yet, this is rarely done in organizations.

Ensure that employees understand why things matter to them: Employees are expected to pay attention to what the leader wants, without understanding why it is meaningful to them and the work. This expectation of blind trust gives the CEO the illusion that what the leader thinks is the only thing that matters. But without employee's attention being focused on the CEOs issue, it won't get the support it needs to be done well. And if the CEO uses force to get what is important to him, the rest of the organization labels the decision as an example of self-interest. This triggers many negative dynamics within the organization. If there isn't authentic active support, there is often open derision about the decision and over time less trust and support in the system. If you want decisions to disappear into the system, to be an integral part of the organization, then you need to ensure that what you are asking is meaningful to people in the organization.

Strategic planning, when not explained in terms of why it matters, causes employees to engage in "creative writing" when asked to explain how their annual goals align with the strategic plan. In other words, they make up answers that have little meaning or weight to them. If we want strategic plans to be actively supported and achieved, we need to make the importance and meaning clear to the individuals in our organizations.

Benefits of using living system dynamics to lead:

Separately and in combination these strategies help me align my leadership with the dynamics of a living system. As more leaders in an organization lead with this living system mindset, the productivity and engagement in the organization shifts towards being a generous system. When I have used these living system dynamics in my consulting practice, I have found that change:

- *Is faster*
- *Is sustainable*
- *Uses less resources and energy*
- *Has significant shared ownership*
- *Uses only the energy it needs*
- *Generates higher quality of results*
- *Benefits from the active engagement of employees*

This kind of change ensures that the solutions disappear into the day-to-day work in organizations. They disappear because leaders from anywhere in the system understand and design their leadership based on the dynamics of how living systems behave.

Questions to Consider:

When we lead with the dynamics of living systems, our results come faster, are more sustainable and cost less to implement. Learning to lead with these dynamics through gentle action and acknowledging that people only accept solutions they help to create are important. When we lead in alignment with these dynamics, the living system will help us and so will the people in the organization. Here are some questions that positional leaders can reflect on and invite discussion on in their teams.

- *Do we communicate why something matters to gain active attention and support by others?*
- *When we initiate change, is it from the top-down?*
- *How is change that bubbles up from the front line, handled in our organization?*
- *Is our model of strategic planning imposed or designed in a way that disappears into the day-to-day work of our employees?*
- *How can we design our work so what we do disappears into the system?*
- *What needs to be explored to ensure our future competitiveness?*
- *What needs to be launched now to take advantage of opportunities or help us fit with our external environment?*
- *What do we want to sustain and maintain from our current body of work?*
- *What do we need to let go of or release to free up resources for new initiatives and innovations?*

CHAPTER ELEVEN

Growing Generous Organizations

> *How do we lead organizations in a way that grows a culture*
> *of a generous organization?*

The answer is to incorporate a developmental mindset in our leadership. If we want our organizations to evolve toward generous systems, we need to intentionally grow our capacity to design and support a generous organization. This chapter focuses on the capabilities that, when they exist in individuals and the organization at large, help our organization become more adaptive and resilient. They create more and consume less—in short, they become generous in design, leadership, and behavior.

Nature doesn't have the same kind of consciousness that individuals do. Therefore, applying the model of generous systems found in nature to organizations must consider how emotions and consciousness can help or hinder its application to human life. For example, the monarch butterfly has already shifted its migration pattern because of climate change. The butterflies didn't need a Paris Climate Agreement to decide to shift their migration behavior, they adapted based on the feedback that they experienced. They accepted feedback from the environment as information; they don't attach an emotional reaction to it.

As humans, our consciousness can cause us to question, evaluate, and disagree with such feedback. Our thinking can be influenced by our feelings about the information. If the feedback aligns with our worldview, we might embrace it. If we fear the information, we may deny it. Our brains and our emotions shape what we see and how we respond.

In this we are different from nature. However, we can still choose to consciously design, grow, and lead our organizations so they respond to feedback and become more like the generous systems found in nature. And along the way, we will be able to design our way out of workplace dysfunction and drama. Because dysfunction and drama is a function of how we lead and the kind of organizational cultures we create.

> *What would a vision of a generous organization look like and what leadership practice would help create and sustain this new type of organization?*

Type I Consumptive Organizations:

In this section, I will articulate what a Type I consumptive organization looks like and what kind of mindset, practices, and capacities would help it evolve toward a Type II consumptive organization.

Initial stages of organizations, like startups or smaller survival-focused businesses or nonprofits gain resources from outside investors or government contracts to drive their work. These sources of support usually aren't very diverse and are dependent on the entrepreneur to deliver on the promise of their potential. As organizations, they tend to be less structured – almost organic, in the way they operate and are led. They are short-lived unless they evolve and invest in their infrastructure. For example, smaller businesses usually have unsophisticated human resource processes, financial analysis, and planning functions. If they grow, their main challenge will be to build stronger infrastructures and management practices to support the growth.

Like the weeds and annuals typical of Type I ecologies in nature, these organizations consume resources from outside investors and give little back until they evolve.

What helps Type I consumptive organizations evolve?

To evolve, the leaders in these organizations need to develop their capacity to be mindful and reflective. The habits that made them successful in this entrepreneurial phase of the business will not help them get to the next stage of evolution.

Another practice that helps small organizations to evolve is to develop a long-time horizon for their decision-making. This requires a worldview shift. They are no longer just surviving for the next quarter or season; they are investing to thrive into the future. This longer time horizon reshapes their decisions and investments.

Leaders can help their organizations evolve by strengthening their individual and collective emotional intelligence. They must learn to manage their emotions, so their decisions are not driven by conscious and unconscious fears. Part of letting go of default behavior is to be conscious of its benefits and limitations. The second part is to manage the emotions of attachment to the default behavior and overcome an emotionally based scarcity mentality. When we become more emotionally intelligent, we learn to recognize the emotions that are driving our defaults and manage them, so they are not mindlessly triggered.

These Type I consumptive organizations also need to find a niche for their product or services that generates sustainable revenues beyond the resources of initial investors. When revenue streams begin to diversify, they can turn an "annual" organization to a "perennial" organization.

Can small startup or family-run businesses be generous organizations?

There are some entrepreneurial enterprises that start out with a design that is like what is found in more mature generous organizations. For example, if the owner has a worldview that sees connection and interdependence. This worldview will influence how they see their employees, customers, and supply lines. They will be more relational and see how investing in their employees will aid in the success of their business.

A client of mine has been in business for about 15 years. When you enter their work environment, there is a feeling of productivity and fun. The employees like working there and feel great about the organization and its purpose. Their benefits and wages reflect an awareness that the business would not be successful without the staff's contributions. The business is not generating profits for the owners on the sacrifices (i.e. low wages) of the employees.

If a small company is designed to run on knowledge as its primary asset, it is easier to link a mindset of connectedness with innovation, services, and knowledge to run more like a generous system. That said, they still will need to confront infrastructure, more sophisticated processes, a stronger data base, and a stronger financial system to grow into a resilient generous organization.

Type II Consumptive Organizations:

In nature, these Type II ecologies start living longer. They still take most of their resources from the soil (think organizational budget) but start investing some of these resources in themselves so they can live longer (over the winter or multiple years). Type II consumptive organizations have crossed the gap from startup to a stronger organization that is supported by the scaffolding of an organizational backroom of finance, technology, facilities, and human resource functions. They also have a stronger leadership structure. However, they are still consumptive because they don't think like a generous system. For example, silos are prominent, and departments and divisions do take organizational resources to invest in the longevity of their specific function. Sometimes this competition between competing divisions can hurt the needs of the larger organization.

For example, they may engage in practices that consume customer's resources and good will such as price gouging on a certain drug that enhances the profits of the organization. Or they may fight against paying a livable wage to their employees because it will impact the size of the company's profit. Or they may extract natural resources, diminishing the environmental commons, or use processes that decrease (consume) the air or water quality because it is more profitable. It is this kind of thinking that makes the collective impact of the organization consumptive.

What helps Type II consumptive organizations evolve?

As our problems become more complex and the connection with the larger environment becomes more robust it triggers a turbulent dynamic within the organization. This disturbance requires the organization to continually adapt (Heifetz, 1994). Like the transition between Type I and Type II consumptive organizations, feedback from the external environment causes leaders to reflect on current practices to see if they still enable the organization to achieve its highest purpose. When an organization continually adapts, it becomes more dynamic, a body in motion tends to stay in motion, supporting its evolution.

Specialization also helps consumptive organizations evolve. As our work becomes more complex we need specialization to focus on various facets of the work. As we specialize, our attention becomes more focused and we need other aspects of the organization to help us with things that we no longer can provide for ourselves. This begins to change our silo mentality. We come to realize that we need to gain the active cooperation of others to help ourselves. Specialization also requires that leadership needs to be spread throughout the organization so these resources are embedded in the specializations, not just at the top of the organization.

This specialization also requires the organization to strengthen its shared higher purpose to hold the whole together instead of being torn apart by competing priorities. Type II consumptive organizations need mindfulness, reflective practice and emotional intelligence to accelerate the shift to generous organizations. They also need to shift their worldview from separation to connection, from closed- systems to open complex and dynamic systems, from short-term time horizon to long-time horizon, and from inert to living systems.

The signs of evolution from consumptive to generous organizations: There are signs of evolution towards generous organizations. We can find them in pockets of large corporations when departments waste less time and energy within their teams and therefore are higher performing and productive. The shift away from disconnected silos toward integrated leadership teams is another sign that we are moving toward generous organizations. When a leadership team starts working together to serve the larger purpose of the company instead of their part of the organization, the company is saying that we need more people leading from the perspective of the whole instead of its part.

I also am encouraged by the growing sophistication of mindfulness and emotional intelligence I see in individual employees. As we build more of this capacity in our organizations, we increase our chances to have it manifest at the organizational level and in our organizational culture.

Developmental Tasks for Leading Generous Organizations

As living systems, organizations have the potential to become generous, but it takes an intentional effort to evolve to be a generous organization. As a manager or positional leader, we rarely are told that our value to our organization is in the development of the people who work there. Usually we are told that our value is to get things done through others. It is our productivity that is measured. In a generous organization, this focus shifts. In addition to helping the organization meet its mission, we also need to help individual employees learn and develop so they and the organization can perform at higher levels and become more like a generous system.

Develop a higher shared purpose for the organization: Nature is organized to ensure the continuation of life on this planet. This purpose is greater than the survival of an individual species. People have a biogenetic need to seek meaning in their work (Kivland, 2017). If we want to grow a generous organization, we need to articulate a higher purpose for the organization that responds to a deep need in the larger society, this has to be more significant than making money or achieving organizational success. For example, Facebook's mission was recently revised to something higher and more important. The original mission was "making the world more open and connected." The revised mission is "to give people the power to build community and bring the world closer together."[9]

Develop a new worldview for the organization and the individuals in the organization: (Allen, 2018). Our worldview shapes the feedback we seek and the way we organize our thoughts. These thoughts and deep background assumptions shape our behaviors. Generous organizations are based in a specific worldview. They assume that we are connected and interdependent and that connections help all of us thrive (Brand, 2008; Capra, 2002; Schein, 2015; Wahl, 2016). Generous systems assume the world is complex and dynamic. It is always in movement and new variables show up every day. Generous systems are open to the wider world. There are no silos in a generous organization. We need to develop an outward mindset where we ask, how can I help others achieve success instead of how can I succeed (The Arbinger Institute, 2016)? Generous organizations have a long-time horizon. They are in the business of thriving over time, not just in the short-term.

These shifts in worldview need to be nurtured in a generous organization. Not everyone will have these mindsets when they are hired. The organization and the leaders within it need to help them develop the deep background assumptions that will reshape their behavior to align with the generous organization we seek to grow.

Individual and organizational reflective practice: To lead generous organizations requires that we develop more mindfulness and organizational consciousness about the way we think and work. There are many defaults that lead us back to being a consumptive organization. To let go of these practices and embrace those of a generous organization, we need to actively reflect on our daily practices both individually and organizationally. When we bring a mindful orientation to our work, we are more focused on learning and getting better.

Recently I had a conversation with a client who actively embraces and experiments with a living system point of view. Despite his consciousness, in this conversation he defaulted to the belief that if change in a system was to happen,

---

[9] (https://www.theverge.com/2017/6/22/15855202/facebook-ceo-mark-zuckerberg-new-mission-statement-groups)

then he was the one who had to make it happen. A living system is always changing, and there are many actors who help the system to change. For a while, my client forgot that and started acting as if he was the only person who could instill change. My client is an active meditator. Once I named his mental starting point, he could consciously reflect on his own thinking and how it was misaligned with his beliefs in living systems and how they operate. This was an example of a reflective practice in action. We need to create cultures that encourage this kind of practice in individuals and the collective organization. Each person who brings more mindful practice to their work, helps the organization collectively reflect on what they are doing and why.

Organizational and individual emotional intelligence: Dysfunction and drama are a direct result of a lack of individual and organizational emotional intelligence. We need to develop the capacity to name feelings and learn to manage them, so they don't spill out and impact others. We all have mirror neurons in our brains that mimic what others are feeling. If we intentionally spread positive energy and emotions that support others and help them gain confidence, we start to activate these mirror neurons and grow a collective intelligence in the organization's culture (Kivland, 2017). We need to expect that our staff will be able to manage their emotions and help the organization do the same.

Assume abundance: Generous organizations are designed to create abundance as in a Type III ecology where the beneficial exchanges between species creates conditions where life can thrive. A consumptive organization assumes scarcity which reinforces the emotions of fear and distrust. Growing generous organizations requires us to notice and be receptive to the abundance that exists (Boldt, 1999).

These days, organizations are focused on creating an innovative culture. In consumptive organizations, we try to control and direct innovation with reward systems and goals and objectives. This is because we think of it as a scarce commodity. If there is a lack of innovation in a consumptive organization, it is because the system doesn't lend itself to receiving the creative talent of its employees. On the other hand, if we assume our organization has an abundance of talent, our job is to unleash it.

See leadership as an emergent property of an organization: Consumptive organizations rely on lone leaders at the top driving the organization. Generous organizations depend on everyone taking the initiative to serve the larger purpose and self-organize their work. Everyone is engaged in a generous organization. Leadership emerges from many individual actions and decisions. In generous organizations, we need to help people see how all their actions contribute to a larger kind of leadership.

Our call to action:

We must see leadership as more than just getting the work done in our organizations. We must develop ourselves, our employees and our organizations. That is our mandate if we want to evolve our organizations beyond consumption and become generous organizations that work for all.

I would love to hear from you and learn from your experience of applying these ideas to your organizational leadership.

Here is my email: keallen1@charter.net and my website www.kathleenallen. net where additional material will be available over time. If you want to sign up for a newsletter or my blog, you can do this on my website.

Questions to Consider

My highest hope for this book is that it is a call to action for leaders at all levels of the organization so that we can help our organizations and teams to evolve toward generous systems. Here are some questions that can focus our conversations and leadership strategies.

- *Where are we along a continuum between highly consumptive and highly generous?*
- *What areas or processes in our organization behave like a generous organization? What can we learn from these examples?*
- *How would we rate our progress towards an emotionally intelligent organization?*
- *How would we rate our progress towards shifting our worldviews to see the world as more connected and interdependent?*
- *How strong is our long-term time horizon?*
- *How mindful are we when we make decisions?*
- *What are small actions that can have the largest impact in accelerating our move towards a generous organization?*
- *What key things do we need to let go of to help us move toward being a generous organization?*

About the Author

Dr. Kathleen Allen is President of her consulting firm, Kathleen Allen and Associates. She has been working in organizations for over twenty-two years and consulting with organizations and leaders for eighteen years.

In her consulting practice, she specializes in leadership coaching and organizational change in human service non-profit organizations, foundations, small to mid-sized businesses, health care, higher educational institutions, and collaborative networks.

Dr. Allen has written and presented widely on topics related to leadership, human development, and organizational development. Dr. Allen is a skilled facilitator of organizational change and organizational development. The earmarks of her work are the creation of shared ownership of the results of a change project, long-term sustainable change for the organization, and increased capacity for the staff members and leaders in those organizations.

She is the author of *Leading from the Roots: Nature Inspired Leadership Lessons for Today's World*. Dr. Allen has co-authored (with Dr. Cynthia Cherrey) *Systemic Leadership: Enriching the Meaning of Our Work*, has written many articles, and contributed to a variety of books including *The Transforming Leader: New Approaches to Leadership for the Twenty-first Century* (Pearson, 2012) and *Innovation in Environmental Leadership: Critical Perspectives* (Redekop, Gallagher, & Satterwhite Eds., 2018).

For the past forty years she has consulted with a wide variety of Foundations in leadership and innovation including W. K. Kellogg Foundation, McKnight Foundation, Surdna Foundation, Sierra Health Foundation, the Blandin Foundation, Sherwood, and others. She has served on the Board of the Leadership Learning Community, and has been a Senior Fellow at the Academy of Leadership at the University of Maryland. Previously she was the Vice President of Student Development at the College of St. Benedict in Minnesota. She has a Doctorate in Leadership from the University of San Diego, CA.

Examples of consulting work include:

- Coaching executives who are instigating cultural change in their organizations.
- Coaching teams, groups of executives, and executive committees of boards of directors who are interested in improving services, strengthening their organization, strengthening their board of directors
- Cultural change initiatives that increase innovation within organizations
- Facilitating collaborative enterprises between non-profit organizations
- Full scale organizational change targeted in shifting the leadership culture from hierarchical leadership to shared or distributive leadership
- Facilitating and designing processes of mergers and acquisitions to help integration of different organizational cultures
- Developing mentoring / staff development programs for employees of a firm
- Consulting with senior leadership teams to improve their learning and leadership capacity

Bibliography

Allen, K. E., Stelzner, S. P., & Wielkiewicz, R. M. (1998). The ecology of leadership: Adapting to the challenges of a changing world. The Journal of Leadership Studies, 5(2), 62-82.

Allen, K. E. (2012). Dancing on a Slippery Floor: Transforming systems, transforming leadership. In Pearson, C. (Ed.). The Transforming Leader: New approaches to leadership for the twenty-first century. (pp. 64-74). San Francisco: Berrett-Koehler Publishers.

Allen, K. E. (2015) Leading Living Systems. TEDX talk https://www.youtube.com/watch?v=DAwHiM-1FnM

Allen, K. E. (2018). Critical Internal Shifts for Sustainable Leadership. In Redekop, B., Gallagher, D.R., & Satterwhite, R. (Eds.). (2018). Innovation in Environmental Leadership: Critical Perspectives. New York & London: Routledge.

Allen, K. E. and Cherrey, C. (2000). Systemic Leadership: Enriching the Meaning of our Work. Washington, D.C.: University Press of America.

Allen, K. E. & Mease, W. P. (2000). Optimizing Energy and Its Role in Leadership. In B. Kellerman & L. R. Matusak Cutting Edge: Leadership 2000. College Park, MD: James Macgregor Burns Academy of Leadership.

Allen, R. (Ed.) (2010). Bulletproof Feathers: How science uses nature's secrets to design cutting-edge technology. Chicago: The University of Chicago Press.

The Arbinger Institute (2016). The Outward Mindset: Seeing beyond ourselves. San Francisco: Berrett-Kohler.

Baker, M. N. (2014). Peer to Peer Leadership: Why the network is the leader. San Francisco: Berrett-Kohler.

Banathy, B. H. (1993). The cognitive mapping of societal system: Implications for education. In Lazzlo, E., & Masulli, I. (Eds.) The Evolution of Cognitive

Maps: New paradigms for the twenty-first century. Amsterdam: Gordon and Breach Science Publishers S. A.

Baumeister, D. (2014). Biomimicry Resource Handbook: A seed bank of best practices. Missoula, MT USA: Biomimicry 3.8.

Benyus, J.M. (2002). Biomimicry: Innovations inspired by nature. New York; Harper Collins.

Boldt, L. (1999), The Tao of Abundance: Eight ancient principles for abundant living. New York: Penguin Group.

Bower, J. L., & C. M. Christensen. "Disruptive Technologies: Catching the Wave." Harvard Business Review 73, no. 1 (January-February 1995): 43-53.

Brafman, O. & Beckstrom, R. A. (2006). The Starfish and the Spider: The unstoppable power of leaderless organizations. New York, Penguin Group.

Brand, S. (2008). The Clock of the Long Now: Time and responsibility. New York, NY: Basic Books.

Brockman, J. (2015). This Idea Must Die: Scientific theories that are blocking progress. New York: Harper Perennial.

Brown, A. (2008). In the Future, the best will be better than perfect: The new biology paradigm. In The Futurists: September-October 2008. 42. (5), 25-28.

Brown, L.D. (1986). Power outside organizational paradigms. In S. Srivastva (Ed.), Executive power: How executives influence people and organizations (pp. 289-311). San Francisco: Jossey-Bass.

Burlingham, B. (2005). Small Giants: Companies that choose to be great instead of big. New York, NY: Penguin Group.

Callenbach, E. (2008). Ecology: A pocket guide (Revised and Expanded). Berkley, CA, University of California Press.

Capra, F. (1996). The web of life. New York: Anchor Books Doubleday.

Capra, F. (2002). The hidden connections: Integrating the biological, cognitive, and social dimensions of life into a science of sustainability. New York: Doubleday.

Carroll, M. (2006). Awake at Work: 35 practical Buddhist principles for discovering clarity and balance in the midst of work's chaos. Boston: Shambhala.

Caspersen, D. (2015). Changing the Conversation: The 17 principles of conflict resolution. New York: Penguin Books

Collins, K. (2014). The Nature of Investing: Resilient investment strategies through biomimicry. Brookline, MA: Bibliomotion, Inc.

Covey, S. (1989). The 7 habits of highly effective people. New York: Simon and Schuster.

Daloz, L. A., Keen, C. H., Keen, J. P., Parks, S. (1996). Common Fire: Lives of commitment in a complex world. Boston: Beacon Press.

Dixon, N. M. (2000). Common Knowledge: How companies thrive by sharing what they know. Boston: Harvard School Press.

Gleick, J. (1987). Chaos: Making a new science. New York: Penguin Books.

Goleman, D. (1995). Emotional Intelligence. New York: Bantam.

Goleman, D. (1997). Working with emotional intelligence. New York: Bantam Books.

Goleman, D., McKee, A., Boyatzis, R. (2002). Primal leadership: Realizing the power of emotional intelligence. Boston: Harvard Business School Press.

Gonzalez, M. (2012). Mindful Leadership: The 9 ways to self-awareness, transforming yourself, and inspiring others. San Francisco: Jossey-Bass.

Gunderson, L. H. & Holling, C. S. (2002). Panarchy: Understanding transformations in human and natural systems. Washington, DC: Island Press.

Hagberg, J.O. (1984). Real power: Stages of personal power in organizations. Minneapolis, MN: Winston Press.

Halal, N. (1998). The Infinite Resource: Creating and leading the knowledge enterprise. San Francisco: Jossey-Bass.

Heifetz, R. (1994). Leadership without easy answers. Cambridge: Belknap Press of Harvard University Press.

Hock, D. (1999). Birth of the Chaordic Age. San Francisco: Berrett-Koehler Publishers.

Hurst, D. K. (2012). The New Ecology of Leadership: Business mastery in a chaotic world. New York: Columbia University Press.

Jennings, P.L. & Dooley, K. J. (2007). An Emerging Complexity Paradigm in Leadership Research. In Hazy, J.K., Goldstein, J.A., Lichtenstein, B.B.

(Eds.). Complex Systems Leadership Theory: New perspectives from complexity science on social and organizational effectiveness. Mansfield, MA: ISCE Publishing.

Johnson, D. W. & Johnson, F. P. (1982). Joining Together: Group Theory and Group Skills Second Edition. Englewood Cliffs, New Jersey: Prentice-Hall, Inc.

Kabot-Zinn, J. (1994). Wherever You Go There You Are: Mindfulness meditation in everyday life. NY: Hyperion

Keller, S. & Price, C. (2011). Beyond Performance: How great organizations build ultimate competitive advantage. New York: Wiley.

Kelly, K. (1998). New Rules for the New Economy: 10 radical strategies for a connected world. New York: Penguin Group

Kiuchi, T. & Shireman, B. (2002) What We Learned in the Rainforest: Business lessons from nature. San Francisco: Berrett-Koehler Publishers.

Kivland, C. (2017). Three Things Employees Want More Than Just Money. White Paper. The Liautaud Institute: University of Illinois at Chicago.

Kohn, A. (1992). No Contest: The case against competition. New York: Houghton Mifflin.

Land, G. (1986). Grow or Die: The unifying principle of transformation. (Reissued Edition). New York: John Wiley & Sons, Inc.

Lencioni, P. (2012). The Advantage: Why organizational health trumps everything else in business. San Francisco: Jossey-Bass.

Lipmanowicz, H. McCandless, K. (2014). The Surprising Power of Liberating Structures: Simple rules to unleash a culture of innovation. Seattle, WA: Liberating Structures Press.

Lyman, A. (2012). The Trustworthy Leader: Leveraging the power of trust to transform your organization. San Francisco: Jossey-Bass.

Lynch, D. & Kordis, P.L. (1988). Strategy of the dolphin: Scoring a win in a chaotic world. New York: William Morrow and Company, INC.

Macy, J. & Johnstone, C. (2012). Active Hope: How to face the mess we're in without going crazy. Novato, CA: New World Library.

McDonough, W. & Braungart, M. (2002). Cradle to Cradle. New York: North Point Press.

McDonough, W. & Braungart, M. (2013). Upcycle: Beyond sustainability designing for abundance. New York: North Point Press.

Meadows, D. H. (2008). Thinking in Systems: A primer. White River Junction, Vermont: Chelsea Green Publishing.

Morgan, A. & Barden, M. (2015). A Beautiful Constraint: How to transform your limitations into advantages, and why it's everyone's business. New York: Wiley.

Muir, J. (1911). My First Summer in the Sierra. New York, NY: Houghton Mifflin.

Negroponte, N. (1995). Being digital. New York: Knopf.

Peat, F. D. (2008). Gentle Action: Bringing creative change to a turbulent world. Grosseto, Italy: Pari Publishing Sas.

Pert, C. B. (1999). Molecules of Emotions. New York: Simon and Schuster.

Quinn, R. E. (2015). The Positive Organization: Breaking free from conventional cultures, constraints, and beliefs. San Francisco: Berrett-Koehler Publishers.

Raelin, J. A. (2010). The Leaderful Fieldbook: Strategies and activities for developing leadership in everyone. Boston, MA: Davies-Black.

Rebeck, G. (2012). Who Really Runs Your Business? Keyhubs Can Show You. In Twin Cities Business Magazine July, 16, 2012.

Rosen, J. (2015). Information Overload. Pp. 315-316. In Brockman, J. (Ed.) (2015). This Idea Must Die: Scientific theories that are blocking progress. New York: Harper Perennial.

Schein, E. H. (1985). Organizational Culture and Leadership. San Francisco: Jossey-Bass.

Schein, S. (2015). A New Psychology for Sustainability Leadership: The hidden power of ecological worldviews. Sheffield 53 8GG, UK: Greenleaf Publishing Limited.

Schmitz, P. (2012). Everyone Leads: Building leadership from the community up. San Francisco: Jossey-Bass.

Senge, P., Kleiner, A., Rovarts, C., Ross, R., and Smith, B. (1994). The Fifth Discipline Fieldbook: Strategies and tools for building a learning organization. New York: Doubleday.

Smart, B. D. (2005). Topgrading: How leading companies win by hiring, coaching, and keeping the best people. NY: Portfolio.

Snowden, D. J. & Boone, M. E. (2007). A Leader's Framework for Decision Making. Harvard Business Review. November.

Stamets, P. (2005). Mycelium Running: How mushrooms can help save the world. Berkeley, CA: Ten speed Press.

Taleb, N. N. (2012). Antifragile: Things that gain from disorder. New York: Random House.

Taleb, N. N. (2007). The Black Swan: The impact of highly improbable fragility. New York: Random House.

Taylor, F. (1915). The Principles of Scientific Management. New York: Harper Brothers Publishers.

Taylor, J., and Wacker, W. (1997). The 500-year delta: What happens after what comes next. New York: Harper Business.

Tazzi, F. (2014). Biomimicry in Organizations: Business management inspired by Nature. CreateSpace Independent Publishing Platform.

Tocqueville, A. (1952). Democracy in America. Oxford, England: Oxford University Press.

Vaill, P. B. (1986). The purposing of high-performing systems. In T. J. Sergiovanni & J. E. Corbally (Eds.), Leadership and Organizational Culture (pp. 85-104). Chicago: University of Illinois Press.

Vecesy, C. & Venables, R.W. (1980). American Indian Environments: Ecological Issues in Native American History. New York: Syracuse University Press.

Wahl, D. C. (2016). Designing Regenerative Cultures. Axminster, England: Triarchy Press.

Walker, B. & Salt, D. (2012). Resilience Practice: Building capacity to absorb disturbance and maintain function. Washington D.C.: Island Press

Wheatley, M. (1992) Leadership and the new science: Learning about organization from an orderly universe. San Francisco: Berrett-Koehler Publishers.

Wheatley, M. & Kellner-Rogers, M. (1996). A Simpler Way. San Francisco: Berrett-Koehler Publishers.

Wurman, R. W. (1989). Information Anxiety. New York: Doubleday.